Armour in Battle:

WAVELL'S OFFENSIVE

Armour in Battle:
WAVELL'S OFFENSIVE

Bryan Perrett

LONDON
IAN ALLAN LTD

First published 1979

ISBN 0 7110 0973 2

Design by Anthony Wirkus LSIAD

Published by Ian Allan Ltd, Shepperton, Surrey; and printed in the United Kingdom by Ian Allan Printing Ltd

Contents

Introduction

Benito Mussolini, de facto ruler of the Italian people, former journalist and sometime corporal of Bersaglieri, declared war on France and Great Britain on 10 June 1940. He did so in the hope that he would share in the German conqueror's spoils, remarking cynically to his Army Chief of Staff, Marshal Pietro Badoglio, that he 'needed a few thousand dead so that he could sit at the conference table as a man who has fought'; and he did so against the advice of his Service Chiefs, who warned him that in their present condition the Italian forces were only capable of fighting a short war, and that it would be 1942 before they could be equipped on a scale suitable for a modern European conflict.

But Benito Mussolini was taking a calculated risk that the war into which he had led his people would be a very short one. France had already been beaten to her knees, and although Britain was preparing to fight for her life, it did not seem likely that she could withstand the might of Germany beyond September.

It was true that in the Middle East General Sir Archibald Wavell commanded some 50,000 British and Imperial troops, but these were stretched thinly across a vast area reaching from the Syrian border to Somaliland. In Egypt itself, the very pivot of British policy in the area, there were only 36,000 men, short of supporting armour and artillery, and it was difficult to see how this small force could menace the 250,000 strong Italian Army in Libya. In Italian East Africa were a further 200,000 men, poised to strike into the Sudan, Kenya and British Somaliland, the largest of whose garrisons numbered only 9,000.

At sea the revitalised Italian Fleet not only enjoyed a wealth of bases in the central Mediterranean, but also outnumbered the British Mediterranean Fleet, although in heavy ships the Royal Navy had a slight advantage, opposing six Italian battleships with seven of their own. In other classes of ship the Italian strength was as disproportionately overwhelming as it seemed on land, 21 cruisers being deployed against eight, 50 destroyers against 37, and 100 submarines against eight. It was not considered to be very important that the Royal Navy had two aircraft carriers in the area, for it had been planned, optimistically, that the Italian Fleet would have the massive support of the land based Reggia Aeronautica, which at the outset could put up about 2,000 aircraft against the RAF and Fleet Air Arm's more or less obsolete types. When Mussolini spoke of the Mediterranean as being *mare nostrum* it did not seem such an idle boast.

The whole area was one of great strategic potential for the Axis Powers, who could exert a stranglehold on, if not actually sever, Britain's shortest trade route to the Far East, and at the same time secure for themselves the precious Middle Eastern oil supplies, once they had broken through Wavell's flimsy screen. After the collapse of France the only Mediterranean bases remaining to Britain were Gibraltar, the small island of Malta and Alexandria; elsewhere the coast belonged either to the enemy or to neutral powers whose attitude varied between the strict impartiality of Turkey and Greece, the sullen indifference of Vichy France and her African colonies, and the thinly veiled hostility of Spain, who had debts to repay to the Fascist dictators who had helped Franco achieve his victory during her Civil War. Spain did, in fact, occupy the International Zone of Tangier on 12 June, thus placing herself in position to close the Straits of Gibraltar if she so wished, and was wooed assiduously by Hitler into either joining the war or at least permitting the passage of troops for an attack on Gibraltar itself.

For Churchill, already fully engaged in rousing the country to prepare for invasion at worst and a long hard struggle at best, the changed situation in the Middle East was the cause of grave anxiety. Splendid *dux bellorum* he might have been, but he was no easy task master, and he bombarded Wavell with a series of signals advising him how best to deploy his limited resources without really understanding what was involved. For his part Wavell, a popular taciturn man given to working out his problems in long periods of detached

thought, resented this constant interference in the running of his command, and relations between the two men became strained. After the Commander-in-Chief had been summoned to London in August, Churchill commented that 'the discussions, both oral and written, were severe'. Nonetheless, neither would permit personalities to cloud the main issue, and with the Battle of Britain approaching its climax, Churchill took the courageous step of despatching three armoured regiments, one equipped with the invaluable Matilda, around the Cape to Egypt, despite the fact that they were desperately needed for home defence.

Churchill might speak grandly of the Army of the Nile or the Army of the Delta, but this was mere rhetoric, for in Egypt Wavell had only the so-far incomplete 7th Armoured Division, the 4th Indian Division and two infantry brigades, one of which was retained permanently for internal security duties among the largely anti-British population. In Palestine the 6th Australian Division was assembling, but even when this was complete the total strength available for use against the Italians in Libya was only that of a weak corps, and never rose above this level.

On the other hand, the quality of the troops was high. Both 7th Armoured and 4th Indian Divisions were regular formations, and the former had reached a high level of training and was quite used to operating in desert conditions; the Indian troops of the latter enjoyed soldiering and were good at it, while about one third of their division consisted of regular British battalions. 6th Australian Division was largely formed from volunteers, big, independent men with their own code of discipline, determined to prove that, like their fathers, they were the best assault infantry in the world.

The Italian Army in Libya might have been expected to be brimming with self-confidence and looking forward to an easy victory. In fact it was not. Since the day after the declaration of war elements of the 7th Armoured Division had harried its frontier garrisons mercilessly and struck deep into its territory, causing in a few weeks no less than 3,000 casualties in exchange for only 150 of its own. So great was the moral ascendency of the light British armoured forces that a German officer on a fact finding mission commented that 'everyone seems scared stiff of the British', echoed by stern Italian affirmations of 'the will to resist', delivered in tones of outraged innocence.

Worse was to follow. On 28 June Marshal Italo Balbo, Commander-in-Chief in Libya, was shot down by his own anti-aircraft gunners over Tobruk. He was succeeded by Marshal Rodolfo

Graziani, who had earned himself a reputation for dash in Ethiopia.

Graziani was under no illusions as to his army's capacity. It was an infantry army and, because it was chronically short of mechanical transport, for the most part it marched and even relied to some extent on pack animals for its supplies. Each infantry division contained an organic tank battalion, but this was equipped with L3 tankettes which could not hope to compete in the tank battle proper. A two-battalion Libyan Tank Group of 70 medium M11/39s was forming, but not only were these tanks badly designed, the formation itself lacked the flexibility of an armoured division. In the artillery morale was high, but the guns were obsolete, many dating back to World War I, and there was a lack of a good anti-tank weapon.

In spite of his reputation for dash and courage, Graziani was a realist with a strong streak of pessimism in his nature. He was obsessed by the logistic difficulties of a desert offensive and, perhaps wisely, he resisted with various excuses all Mussolini's attempts to get him to invade Egypt. On 8 August he was in Rome and prophetically told Count Ciano, the Italian Foreign Minister and the Duce's son-in-law, 'The water supply is entirely insufficient. We move towards a defeat which, in the desert, must inevitably develop into a total disaster.' But Mussolini badly wanted a victory to boast about and, losing patience with Graziani, told him that unless he commenced his offensive forthwith, he would be relieved.

With great reluctance, therefore, the Marshal crossed the frontier on 13 September, taking four days to cover the 60 miles to Sidi Barrani, just half way to the main British position at Mersa Matruh. After establishing an advanced post at Maktila he refused to go further, and established a chain of fortified camps stretching away south-west towards the distant escarpment. Nothing could persuade him to continue the advance, for which he insisted he required more tanks, guns, reinforcements and supplies.

As the weeks went by events elsewhere began to take a hand. On 4 October Hitler and Mussolini met at the Brenner Pass. Hitler expressed himself well pleased with Italian dominance in the Mediterranean, and Mussolini returned to Rome determined to spur Graziani to fresh endeavours. Almost at once he was told of the German occupation of Rumania, of which Hitler had kept him in ignorance. Furious at being treated as a nonentity, Mussolini decided to prove to the world that he was quite as capable of taking such initiatives on his own account, and announced that he was going to 'occupy' Greece.

This was not a calculated risk; it was lunacy. The Greeks has no intention of being occupied, and when the Italians invaded on 28 October they met with ferocious resistance. Within weeks they had been thrown back into Albania, where they suffered one defeat after another. It goes almost without saying that the forces employed in this arid and illogical venture might, perhaps, have been used more profitably by Graziani in Egypt. On the night of 11/12 November the Fleet Air Arm crippled the Italian battle fleet in Taranto harbour. For the British this dramatic change in the naval balance meant, among other considerations, that the Army would have the support of the Royal Navy's 15-inch gun battleships and other warships in its operations; for the Italian soldier within range the effect of naval gunfire would produce an unimaginable experience of terror and destruction which smothered his will to fight.

The idea of a spoiling attack against the Italians had been in Wavell's mind almost as soon as they began to settle into their fortified camps. He envisaged a simple raid, lasting perhaps four or five days and designed to disrupt the enemy's preparations for a continued advance, and the arrival of the three fresh armoured regiments and aircraft reinforcements, flown across Africa from the Gold Coast, gave the plan a real chance of success.

Meanwhile, Churchill had become restive again and, convinced that Wavell was more interested in the situation in East Africa than in the Mediterranean, despatched his Secretary of State for War, Anthony Eden, to Egypt in early October. Wavell, perhaps feeling that a fait accompli was the best way to handle the politicians, told neither of his plans and complied with their directive to send limited aid to Greece.

However, when Churchill cabled in early November that the Greek theatre held absolute priority, Wavell felt that he must disclose what he had in mind, and Eden returned to London with the details. The Prime Minister was immediately enthusiastic and, although he was angry at being kept in the dark for so long, he gave the project his full support, encouraging Wavell to pursue even more ambitious objectives.

With Gen Maitland Wilson, Commander-in-Chief of the British troops in Egypt, and Maj Gen Richard O'Connor, commander of the Western Desert Force based on Mersa Matruh, Wavell put the finishing touches to his plan. Training continued in great secrecy throughout November, and on 9 December the raid itself was mounted under the codename of Operation Compass. The raid resulted in a shattering defeat for the Italians, and its success was exploited ruthlessly by O'Connor. Within two months and at a cost of only 2,000 casualties, Wavell's 'Thirty Thousand' smashed an army of 10 divisions, took over 130,000 prisoners, captured nearly 400 tanks and 1,000 guns and occupied half of Libya. Wavell had won a complete and crushing victory against impossible odds, and if to Churchill it seemed little short of miraculous, to Benito Mussolini it was utterly inexplicable.

How it came about forms the story of this book.

Diary of Major Events in 1940 Relating to the Middle Eastern Theatre of War prior to Operation Compass

3 June	Dunkirk evacuation ends
10 June	Italy declares war on France and Great Britain
11 June	7th Armoured Division commences harassing operations against Italian troops along the Egyptian-Libyan frontier
12 June	Spain declares herself non-belligerent, but occupies the International Zone of Tangier two days later, and is thus in a position to close the Straits of Gibraltar
21 June	Italians advance into France
22 June	France signs armistice with Germany
24 June	France signs armistice with Italy
3 July	French naval squadron at Oran destroyed by the Royal Navy to prevent its use by the Axis Powers Other French warships in British ports taken over
4 July	Vichy French Government breaks off diplomatic relations with Great Britain
9 July	British and Italian battle fleets engage. Italian fleet retires, having sustained some damage, and claims a victory
10 July	Battle of Britain begins
13 July	Italians take the border town of Moyale in Kenya
16 July	Hitler orders that plans for Operation Sealion, the invasion of Britain, must be completed by mid-August
3 August	Italians invade British Somaliland
19 August	British withdraw from Somaliland
20 August	Italy announces a total blockade of British possessions in the Mediterranean and Africa
13 September	Italians invade Egypt, capturing Sollum
17 September	The Luftwaffe concedes defeat in the Battle of Britain. Operation Sealion postponed
18 September	Italian army reaches Sidi Barrani
2 October	The Royal Navy shells the Dodecanese Islands
4 October	Hitler and Mussolini meet at the Brenner Pass
23 October	Hitler meets Franco to discuss Spain's entry into the war and the possibility of an attack on Gibraltar
28 October	Italians invade Greece
29 October	British troops sail for Crete
6 November	British capture of Gallabat on the Sudan front
11/12 November	Fleet Air Arm torpedo bomber attack cripples the Italian battle fleet at Taranto
14 November	Greeks push Italians back into Albania
22 November	Italian IX Army routed by Greeks at Koritsa
1- 8 December	Further Greek victories
9 December	Operation Compass begins

Diary of Major Events Following Commencement of Operation Compass

9 December 1940	7th Armoured Division isolates Sidi Barrani 4th Indian Division storms fortified camps at Nibeiwa and Tummar Maktila attacked by Selby Force
10 December	Sidi Barrani stormed. Italians abandon Maktila
11 December	Italians abandon fortified camps at Rabia and Sofafi 4th Indian Division withdrawn from Western Desert Force
12 December	7th Armoured Division continues pursuit. Rearguard action at Buq Buq
17 December	Sollum re-occupied
Late December	6th Australian Division assembles on Frontier. Franco decides that Spain will remain neutral
3- 5 January 1941	6th Australian Division storms Bardia
21-22 January	6th Australian Division storms Tobruk
28 January	Italians abandon Wadi Derna line
5 February	7th Armoured Division establishes road-block at Beda Fomm
6 February	Heavy fighting at Beda Fomm. Australians enter Benghazi
7 February	Italian Army surrenders at Beda Fomm

Wavell and his Commanders

General (later Field Marshal) Sir Archibald Wavell, Commander-in-Chief, Middle East (*Below*).

Born in 1883, Wavell followed his father into the Black Watch, with whom he fought as a subaltern during the Boer War. After a further period of active service on the North-West Frontier, he went to France in 1914 and was present during the First Battle of Ypres as Brigade Major 9th Infantry Brigade. The following year he was awarded the Military Cross and was wounded at the Second Battle of Ypres, losing his left eye. 1916 found him serving as Military Attache to the Grand Duke Nicholas, commander of the Russian Army of the Caucasus, being made a member of the Orders of St Vladimir and St Stanislaus. For the remainder of the war he served in Palestine under Allenby, whom he greatly admired. By 1919 he had reached the rank of Brigadier General Staff with XX Corps, but the inevitable reduction of the Army meant a return to his substantive rank of Major, and in 1920 he rejoined his regiment as a company commander, although he was promoted the following year. His first book, *The Palestine Campaign*, appeared in 1928. By 1930 he was a Brigadier again, commanding 6th Infantry Brigade at Aldershot. Promotion to Major-General followed in 1933 and in this rank he wrote Volume II of *Field Service Regulations* before returning to Aldershot in 1935 to command 2nd Infantry Division. After attending the 1936 Red Army manoeuvres he became GOC Palestine and Transjordan in 1937. He was promoted Lieutenant-General the following year and appointed GOC Southern Command. In 1939 he was posted to Egypt as GOC-in-C Middle East, having been made a Knight Commander of the Bath, the same year seeing the appearance of his book *Generals and Generalship*. His appointment of Commander-in-Chief Middle East was confirmed in 1940, his local rank of General being made substantive on 1 October the same year.

His relationship with Churchill was never good, and after the failure of Operation Battleaxe and the campaign in Greece, the Prime Minister removed him from command and he took up the appointment of Commander-in-Chief India, which he held until 1943. During the period of Japanese expansion he was Supreme Commander ABDA (American British Dutch Alliance). In 1943 he became Viceroy and Governor-General of India. He died on 24 May 1950. / *IWM*

O'Connor

Left: Wavell's executive field commander was Lt-Gen R. N. O'Connor, to whom the credit must be awarded for bringing the campaign to such a spectacularly successful conclusion. O'Connor's regiment was The Cameronians (Scottish Rifles) and like many light infantry officers, including Guderian, he had an instinctive grasp of the principles of mechanised warfare. However, unlike Guderian, he had not been influenced by writers who had set down the theories of Blitzkrieg in the interwar years, and considers that in the circumstances his tactics were simply dictated by logic, commenting that 'had they been incorrect, the Italians would have fought a great deal better, slowed up our advance, and given us much heavier casualties. Surprise in every form was what the Italians disliked'.

During World War I he had been awarded the DSO and bar, the Military Cross, the Italian Silver Medal for Valour, and had been mentioned in despatches no less than nine times. He commanded the important Peshawar Brigade on the North-West Frontier between 1936 and 1938 and then took over the post of Military Governor of Jerusalem, which he held on the outbreak of war.

For his part in the campaign he was made a Knight Commander of the Bath, but was captured in April 1941 during Rommel's first North African offensive. He succeeded in escaping in December 1943 and commanded VIII Corps during the fighting in Normandy. / *IWM*

Hobart

Right: Maj-Gen P. C. S. Hobart had begun his military career in the Bengal Sappers and Miners, and had later transferred to the then Tank Corps. He had been closely involved with the British Army's early experimental armoured formations and arrived in Egypt in 1938 to command the Mobile Division, which later grew into 7th Armoured Division. As a result of his methods the division was trained to a very high standard and fully acclimatised for desert warfare. His combined energy and enthusiasm for armour amounted to something like genius, but he could be insultingly rude, was no respecter of persons and was intolerant of anyone who did not accept his ideas immediately. Neither Wavell nor Lt-Gen Maitland Wilson, local commander of the British troops in Egypt, found him an easy subordinate and both felt, a little unfairly, that his ideas centred on the tank to the virtual exclusion of all other arms, a situation which they did not consider to be acceptable. In September 1939 Hobart was removed from command and left the Army. He was serving as a junior NCO in the Home Guard when Churchill rescued him, and he later raised and trained the 11th and 79th Armoured Divisions, commanding the latter in Europe.

Graziani's crushing defeat led to much talk of the British having a 'natural affinity' for the desert; this was simple minded nonsense. If Wavell's troops lived, fought and maintained themselves with less difficulty than the Italians it was because they had been trained to do so in a hard school — Hobart's. / *IWM*

O'Moore Creagh

Above left: Maj-Gen Sir Michael O'Moore Creagh, commander of 7th Armoured Division. Creagh was a cavalryman who had served in the 7th and later the 15th/19th Hussars. During World War I he won the Military Cross and was mentioned in despatches. He was made a Knight of the British Empire for his services during the 1940/41 operations against the Italians, but left the division following the failure of Operation Battleaxe. This photograph was taken shortly before he retired from the Army to join UNRRA in 1944. / *IWM*

Beresford-Peirse

Above: Maj-Gen Sir Noel Beresford-Peirse, KBE, CB, DSO, was born in 1887 and commissioned into the Royal Artillery. After the capture of Sidi Barrani, his 4th Indian Division was sent to Eritrea, where it fought with distinction before returning to the Western Desert. Beresford-Peirse commanded XIII Corps during the abortive Battleaxe operations but was removed during the subsequent purge and appointed GOC Sudan. He later commanded XV Corps in India. / *IWM*

Mackay

Left: Maj-Gen Sir Iven Mackay, KBE, commanding 6th Australian Division. Like a number of senior Australian commanders Mackay was not a professional soldier but had seen active service in World War I. He commanded 4th Infantry Battalion during 1916/17, and subsequently 1st Machine Gun Battalion. When the Great War ended he was commanding 1st Australian Infantry Brigade. In common with O'Moore Creagh and Beresford-Peirse he was knighted shortly after Beda Fomm. He is seen here reviewing his division. / *IWM*

The Frontier War and the Italian Invasion of Egypt

Below: With the carrying of respirators the only concession to hostilities, this column of British infantry shows all the spit and polish of garrison soldiering. However, once the fighting began, sun helmets and starched khaki drill soon gave way to more practical clothing. / *IWM*

Bottom: Nonetheless, training for desert war was taken very seriously, and the majority of units were thoroughly acclimatised to its demanding conditions before the Italian declaration of war. This photograph, taken during an exercise in mid-1940, shows Light Tanks of 7th Armoured Division acting in the infantry support role in the absence of more substantial vehicles. Infantry support was the province of the purpose-built Matildas, but at this stage there were none in the Middle East. / *IWM*

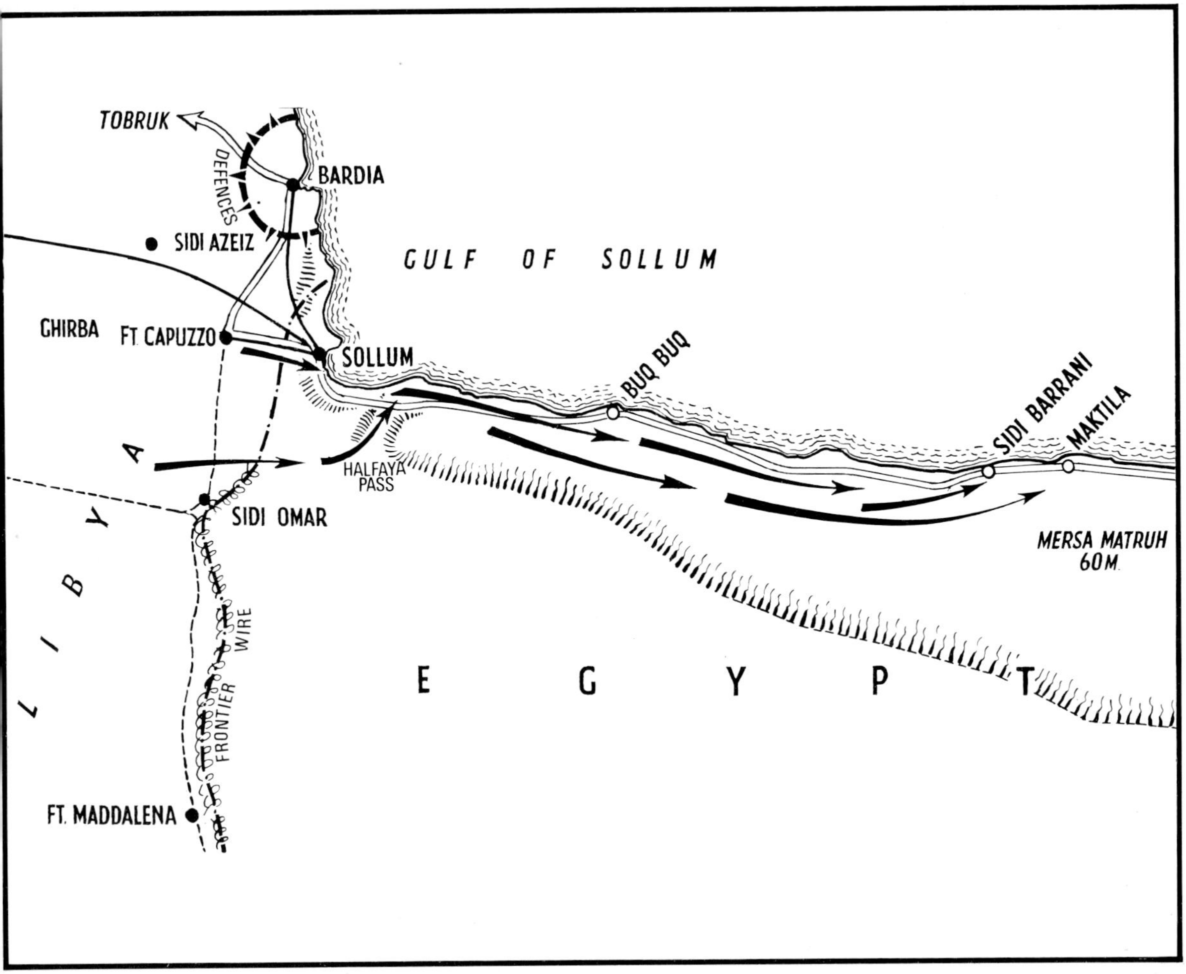

Above: The Frontier War and the Invasion of Egypt.

Left: The 11th (Prince Albert's Own) Hussars were 7th Armoured Division's armoured car regiment and were equipped with 1924-pattern Rolls-Royce and Morris armoured cars. The Italian declaration of war found all three squadrons lying close to the Frontier Wire, which they were ordered to cross with instructions to raise hell, in the broadest possible sense, beyond. It was a role for which the regiment, under the command of Lt-Col John Combe, was temperamentally well suited.

Combe had foreseen that the Wire would have to be crossed sooner or later, and his cars had practised doing this on a specially constructed replica. The best method was found to be a slow, steady push which stretched the wire to its limits and eventually caused it to part under pressure from the armoured flaps which covered the car's radiator.

Apart from its armament, which consisted of a Boys anti-tank rifle and a Bren light machine gun, the Rolls-Royce armoured car differed little from those of the Duke of Westminster's armoured car company which had fought the Senussi on exactly the same ground in 1916. On good going the Rolls-Royce could achieve 45mph. / *IWM*

Right: Beyond the Wire, the Italians had established a chain of desert forts, in the manner of the French Foreign Legion. Although equipped with artillery, machine guns, searchlights and sometimes surrounded by a wired perimeter minefield, the only military benefit they provided was to impress the local tribesmen, and they had no capacity to withstand shellfire or bombing. The principal forts were Capuzzo, Sidi Omar and Maddalena. Their potential was summed up by the ferocious eagle at Capuzzo which glared towards the Egyptian frontier; the bird was made from plaster, as was its plinth, which was also hollow. / *IWM*

Below: The declaration of war had little immediate impact on the routine of the Italian frontier garrisons, whose vehicles continued to use full headlights after dark. During the night of 11 June a convoy of four lorries bound for Sidi Omar drove into an 11th Hussar ambush set by Lt Miller, and after a short exchange of fire two Italian officers and 50 Libyan soldiers surrendered, the former protesting violently against the use of 'neutral' Egyptian territory as a base for aggressive action. They are seen here being marched into a POW compound under an escort which would in later days be regarded as excessive./ *IWM*

Below: The incident had an immediate effect. On 13 June a Hussar patrol probed the enemy position at Sidi Omar, consisting of two small adjacent forts, to find it deserted and partially gutted. In view of the small forces they were employing along the frontier the British were beginning to sense that already the Italians had no heart for the fight. / *IWM*

Bottom: The same day a two-car troop tried to drive straight into Fort Maddalena, but was repulsed by heavy machine gun fire, and assailed in turn by no less than six Caproni bombers and nine Fiat fighters. The cars were able to take evasive action and emerged unscathed, although they had been under attack for over an hour.

On 14 June the whole of A Squadron 11th Hussars was detailed to attack the fort again, supported this time by a squadron of Blenheims. Most of the garrison had already left by the time the bombers arrived overhead, and after the bombs had fallen the remainder surrendered to the Hussars after a token resistance. The fort was found to contain 'a high class barracks, an electric light plant and a refrigerator, a garage, an underground water tank, and an 80-foot observation tower'.

This further abandonment and the daily attacks of hostile aircraft made it clear that Italian policy was to hold the frontier zone with the Reggia Aeronautica rather than with ground troops. / *IWM*

Right and below: In spite of its elderly appearance the Fiat CR42 Falco entered service in 1939. The aircraft was armed with one 7.7mm and one 12.7mm Breda, fitted above the forward fuselage. With a top speed of 267mph it was slightly faster than the Gladiator, but had a comparable ceiling, and was equally manoeuvrable. A group of 50 took part in the Battle of Britain, sustaining heavy losses. The CR42 was the most numerous fighter possessed by the Reggia Aeronautica in North Africa. This example was shot down near Buq Buq.

The Fiat G50 monoplane fighter had seen service during the Spanish Civil War and had a maximum speed of 293mph and an operational ceiling of 32,800ft. It was armed with two 12.7mm Breda machine guns housed in the forward fuselage, one of which can clearly be seen in this example, which seems to have been the victim of ground strafing. Throughout the campaign more Italian aircraft were destroyed on the ground than in aerial combat. / *IWM*

Right: The most modern fighter in the Reggia Aeronautica's arsenal was the Macchi C200 Saetta (Thunderbolt), which could out-climb and out-manoeuvre the Hurricane, although its 312mph maximum speed was slightly slower and its operational ceiling of 29,000ft substantially less. Although armed only with two 12.7mm machine guns fitted above the cowling, the Saetta had a good combat record and its pilots often more than held their own against British aircraft. The C200 was powered by a Fiat 860hp engine. / *IWM*

Above: When Italy declared war, the Royal Air Force in Egypt could muster a handful of Gladiator fighters, some Blenheim light bombers, and a few Wellington and Bombay medium bombers. From the outset this tiny force pursued an aggressive policy of attacking the enemy's airfields, the base at El Adem being raided on the first day of the war.

The Gloster Gladiator was a single seater biplane fighter powered by a Bristol Mercury 840hp engine giving a maximum speed of 253mph and an operation ceiling of 33,000ft. It was armed with four .303in Browning machine guns, two in the fuselage and one under each lower wing. While old fashioned in design, this highly manoeuvrable aircraft remained in service until 1942. At one stage Malta's fighter defence consisted of a flight of three Gladiators, named *Faith*, *Hope* and *Charity*.

The Bristol Blenheim light bomber carried a bomb load of 1,000lb and was armed with a fixed machine gun in the nose and either one or two machine guns in the dorsal turret. The aircraft was driven by two Bristol Mercury 840hp engines. Maximum speed was 266mph and operational ceiling 31,500ft. The Blenheim had a range of 1,950miles. / *IWM*

Below: Carriers of 1st Battalion King's Royal Rifle Corps at Fort Capuzzo, which was also attacked on 14 June. Capuzzo covered the approach to the fortress of Bardia from the British frontier position at Sollum, and was regarded as a key feature of the Italian defence system. It was expected to offer more serious resistance than Maddalena, as was the fortified camp at Sidi Azeiz some way to the north.

Brig Caunter's 4th Armoured Brigade was detailed to attack both Capuzzo and Sidi Azeiz with RAF support, and after a short duel between 7th Hussars' cruisers and the defending artillery, the fort surrendered before the mechanised KRRC company could launch its attack.

At Sidi Azeiz, however, the Italians succeeded in holding their own against the 7th's light tanks and the 11th's armoured cars. / *IWM*

Bottom: As C Squadron 11th Hussars withdrew from Sidi Azeiz they were attacked by a company of L3 light tanks. After an anti-tank rifle had knocked out one of their number, the Italians withdrew, and the crew of the casualty were quickly captured while their vehicle was set on fire. Thereafter the L3s were regarded as being little more than a nuisance, barely capable of competing with armoured cars. This Hussar Morris is shown towing one home as a trophy. / *IWM*

Left: On 15 June an 11th Hussar patrol snapped up a staff car containing a portly engineer general and his two lady companions. The general was carrying a detailed set of plans of the Bardia defences, which were put to good use later in the campaign.

The following day the armoured cars intercepted two convoys of lorried infantry accompanied by four guns and a company of L3s. After two of the Italians' light tanks had been knocked out, the column formed square with the lorried infantry in the centre, light tanks on the flanks, and a gun at each corner. These tactics, suitable for a night leaguer in hostile tribal territory, were suicidal when employed as a defence against a fully mechanised enemy with ample firepower at his disposal.

Brig Caunter had despatched a troop of 2-pdr anti-tank guns and a squadron of 7th Hussars to assist the Eleventh, but by the time the tanks arrived breakdowns had reduced their number to two cruisers and three lights. The Italian tank commander, himself a former cavalryman, fully appreciated the incongruity of his situation and led his L3s in a counter-attack that was gallantly pressed home. One of the Seventh's cruisers found an L3 hanging grimly on to its tail, blazing away with its machine guns until the larger tank increased speed sufficiently for the 2-pdr to be depressed over the engine deck and a round sent into the little vehicle. One by one the remaining L3s were knocked out; the photograph shows one that has been reduced to its component parts by an internal explosion. / *IWM*

Right: Having disposed of their opponents, the British tanks and armoured cars circled the square, raking it through and through with their fire. The Italian gun crews fought until shot down around their weapons, but the infantry broke and tried to escape across the desert in their lorries, with the 11th Hussars in hot pursuit; those that did not surrender were harried until their vehicles were burning wrecks.

Col D'Avanzo, commander of the force which had been so dramatically annihilated, was shot dead in his car, and on his body were found orders stating that 'You will destroy enemy elements which have infiltrated across the frontier, and give the British the impression of our decision, ability and will to resist.'

Not a single British casualty had been incurred during the so-called Battle of Ghirba. The Italian survivors, numbering seven officers and 94 men, about a third of the original force, were herded back across the frontier along with the captured guns and a solitary L3, under tow. / *IWM*

Right: A10 Cruisers on good going. Throughout June and July each of 7th Armoured Division's four armoured regiments (7th and 8th Hussars, 1st and 6th Royal Tank Regiments) was engaged in operations across the frontier. With each success confidence rose, although by the end of July it was clear that the old free-wheeling days were over, for the Italians had begun employing heavy columns protected by artillery and anti-tank guns and with tank and air support on call, to dominate the Capuzzo sector. On 25 July an 11th Hussar patrol, detailed to raid the Bardia/Tobruk road, failed to return, the cars having been shot up from the air and the survivors rounded up by tanks. The Italians chivalrously dropped a list of the prisoners they had taken and an account of the engagement on to 7th Armoured Division's Headquarters, during an air attack. / *IWM*

Centre left: On 5 August 8th Hussars were involved in an inconclusive action with a battalion of M11 medium tanks between Capuzzo and Sidi Azeiz. Thereafter, the frontier lapsed into several weeks of comparative inactivity as Graziani made plans for his offensive.

Air attacks by the Reggia Aeronautica continued, however, with British forward units being bombed and straffed regularly. This RTR squadron, seen in a semi-permanent leaguer area, has protected suspensions and vulnerable side plating against aircraft fire by constructing small sangars where it has not been possible to dig in the tanks. / *IWM*

Bottom left: An A13 crew at maintenance, with their brew bubbling on the tank cooker to the right. Normal out-of-contact routine following reveille would be the heating of a small quantity of water for washing and shaving, in which the crew took turns, following which one member would prepare breakfast while the others packed up and stowed bedding and bivouac sheets and went through the sequence of pre-running checks.

By now, mechanical failures were beginning to take their toll of 7th Armoured Division's cruisers, only half of which were available for action at any one time. / *IWM*

Above: As the division represented Egypt's first line of defence, Wavell saw no point in its continuing to wear itself down in small operations along the frontier, and withdrew both armoured brigades for a refit in anticipation of the expected Italian offensive.

In any one mile of running the wear on a tank's tracks, running gear and transmission is far greater than that sustained by a wheeled vehicle, and to eliminate as much mileage as possible tanks are carried on specially constructed transporters whenever circumstances permit. / *IWM*

Left: A13s on patrol. Following the departure of the armoured brigades, only a single squadron of tanks remained on the frontier, although 11th Hussars' armoured cars were still active and 7th Armoured Division's Support Group provided a pivot of manoeuvre. / *IWM*

Right: A dug in 25-pdr of 7th Armoured Division's Support Group, which consisted of 4th Royal Horse Artillery, 1st Battalion King's Royal Rifle Corps and 2nd Battalion The Rifle Brigade, with anti-tank defence provided by the 2-pdr and 37mm Bofors guns of 3rd Royal Horse Artillery. The function of the Support Group was to provide a firm base for the operations of the armoured brigades, as well as artillery fire support.

Possibly the Support Group's most famous soldier was Lt-Col Jock Campbell, commanding 4 RHA, who would within weeks be leading the mobile columns of armoured cars, guns and lorried infantry that would carry his name — the Jock Columns. As a Brigadier he was awarded the Victoria Cross while commanding the Support Group during Operation Crusader. / *IWM*

Above: The first three months of the war saw 3,500 casualties inflicted on the Italians at a cost of only 150 to the British. In addition, large quantities of equipment, such as these AA/anti-tank guns, had been captured. Of even greater importance was the tremendous moral ascendency which the fighting on the frontier had given the British over their opponents. British command of the desert and the constant baiting attacks not only caused the Italians to lose confidence in themselves, and consequently the will to win, but also caused them to magnify the strength of Western Desert Force to a scale well beyond Wavell's resources. Senior German officers visiting North Africa found their allies nervous and depressed. The poor quality of Italian equipment spoke for itself, but there was also a serious leadership problem, which was aggravated by political preferment within the officer corps. While the Germans considered that most of the Italian commanders were capable men, the distant relationship between officers and men at regimental level drew unfavourable comment. The Italian officer was a privileged individual who lived and ate separately from his men, receiving better rations even when in the field, and leaving his NCOs to look after the welfare of his command. Hardships were thus unevenly shared, and in consequence no sense of respect or comradeship could be developed, and the men were often unwilling to respond to critical situations.

Nor did it escape German attention that the average Italian was not a willing soldier, but it was felt that even allowing for this, and his volatile nature, good leadership could have turned him into a tough and dedicated fighter. Numerous examples of individual heroism confirm this view, particularly among the artillery and those armoured units raised from former cavalry regiments, which had a totally different esprit from the rest of the Army. / *IWM*

Top left: Perhaps one of the strangest pieces captured was this 12-pdr mountain gun, designed for a very different environment than the open desert where its short range can have been of little use. / *IWM*

Centre left: For their part the series of minor actions had caused the British to realise that the Italian Army might be strong in numbers, but that it was also very poorly equipped. These 11th Hussars are examining an Italian version of the famous French Seventy-Five, still on the type of carriage used during World War I. / *IWM*

Below: When, at last, Graziani did order a move into Egypt, the fact was proudly and prematurely announced by Rome radio. After seizing Sollum, garrisoned by a single platoon, and the Halfaya Pass, his advance guard continued ponderously along the coast road, each phase heralded by a bombardment of the empty desert ahead, while the Italian tanks sought to hold off the attacks of the apparently ubiquitous Support Group. Graziani's persistent fears that his marching columns would be overwhelmed by an avalanche of British armour were quite groundless, for only 11th Hussars and one squadron of 1 RTR were operating in the area. On the night of 16 September the British rearguard neatly disengaged and retired through Sidi Barrani to the main defensive position at Mersa Matruh. / *Keystone Press Agency Ltd*

Above: Bersaglieri probe their way cautiously into an abandoned village. Four days after beginning his offensive, Graziani reached Sidi Barrani and, after establishing an advanced post at Maktila, curtailed any further forward movement.

Casualties had amounted to only 120 killed and 410 wounded, but the infantry were exhausted and the tanks had begun to suffer breakdowns at an alarming rate. Graziani felt that he could not risk a further advance until he received substantial reinforcements, particularly of mechanical transport, and began to construct a series of fortified camps stretching south-west towards the escarpment.

Sidi Barrani was a tiny coastal village, but Rome radio could not resist the urge to over-capitalise on the small success of its capture, proclaiming that the 'town' was now quiet, and that tramcars were once again running normally in its streets! / *Keystone Press Agency Ltd*

Top right: The crippling blow sustained by the Italian Navy at Taranto meant that units of Admiral Sir Andrew Cunningham's Mediterranean Fleet could be spared to support the Army's operations in North Africa. Here cruisers are seen engaging Italian positions along the coast. / *IWM*

Right: Ample evidence of the firepower available is provided by this photograph of the battleships *Malaya* and *Ramillies* (*Malaya* leading) en route to a coastal bombardment. Both ships carried a main armament of eight 15-inch guns, and belonged respectively to the Queen Elizabeth and Royal Sovereign class. In the background is the County class cruiser *Kent*, while overhead circles a Swordfish, the type of aircraft which delivered the attack on Taranto. / *IWM*

The principal British defence line was at Mersa Matruh, and was hastily constructed with whatever materials were to hand. Entrenchments revetted with sandbags, such as this mortar pit, and lines of concrete dragon's teeth and girder hedgehogs, offered no defence against a mobile force prepared to penetrate the desert to the south. Nor could this emplaced Vickers Medium tank turret with its 3-pdr gun and water-coooled mg exercise anything more than a local influence. The real strength of the defences lay in the presence of 7th Armoured Division as a counter-attack force. However, the position was never put to the test, as the Italian advance halted some 60 miles away. / *IWM*

Operation Compass

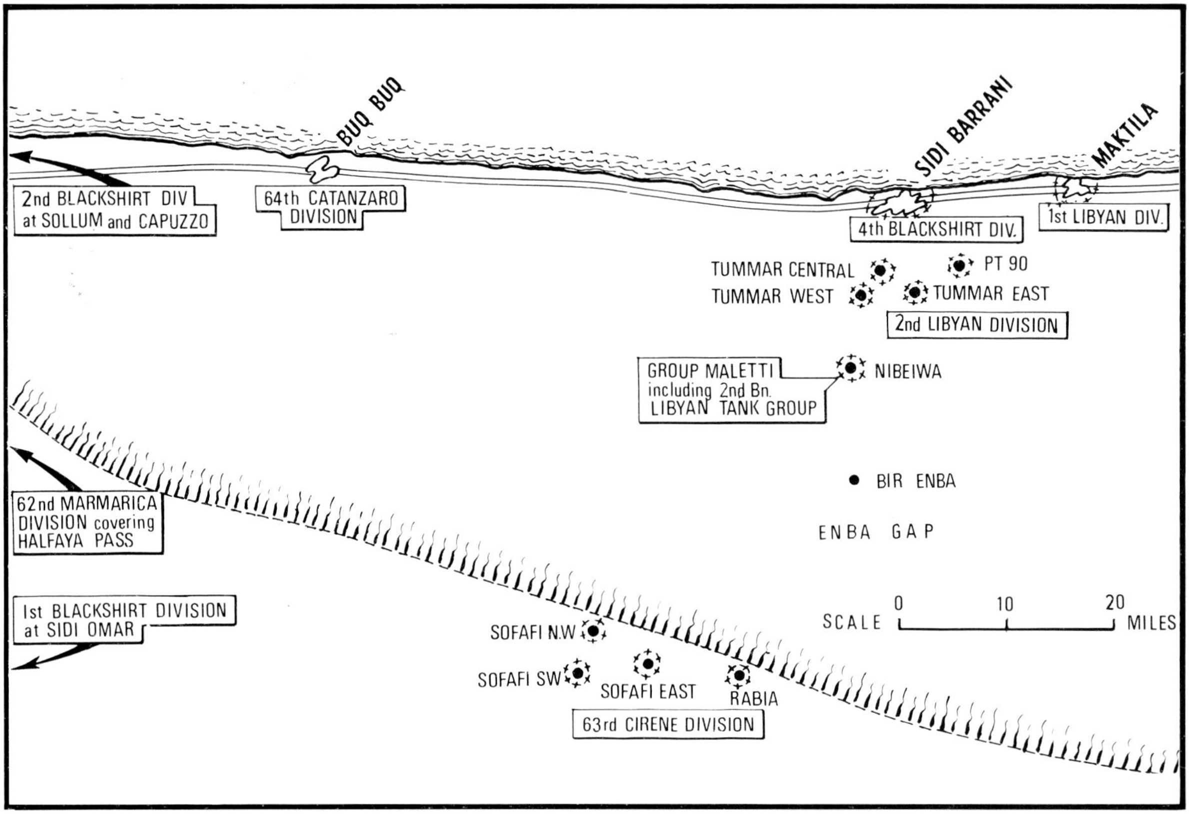

Above: Italian dispositions in Egypt prior to Operation Compass. A fatal flaw in the Italian dispositions south of Sidi Barrani was the Enba Gap, a 20 mile unprotected stretch of desert lying between the fortified camps of Nibeiwa and Rabia. In this area British columns of armoured cars, artillery and lorried infantry, known as Jock Columns after their originator, Brig Jock Campbell, soon established the sort of domination that had existed in the early days along the frontier. Not surprisingly, when Wavell and O'Connor decided to mount Operation Compass, designed simply as a five-day raid, the Enba Gap was chosen as a back door into the heart of the Italian positions in preference to an advance along the coast where the enemy was strongest.

Right: By the end of September an air ferry route had been established across Africa from the Gold Coast to Egypt, and the first modern Hurricane fighters were beginning to arrive. This photograph, taken days before the start of Operation Compass, illustrates graphically how the almost universal 'vic' of three had given way to the more flexible 'finger-four' formation developed during the Battle of Britain.

In various forms the Hawker Hurricane single-seater fighter saw service in almost every theatre of war, including the Eastern Front. Those used by the RAF against the Reggia Aeronautica in 1940/41 had a maximum speed of 322mph and a service ceiling of 36,000ft, and were equipped with eight wing-mounted .303in Browning machine guns. The 1,030hp V-12 Rolls-Royce Merlin engine could produce a climbing rate of 2,520ft/min. / *IWM*

Top: In early October reinforcements — three armoured regiments despatched round the Cape from the United Kingdom — began to arrive in Egypt. They were 3rd King's Own Hussars with light tanks, 2 RTR with cruisers and 7 RTR with Matildas. This A13 cruiser of 2 RTR still carries the tactical markings of 1st Armoured Division, the regiment's former parent formation in England. Another point of interest is the type of 'roll-up' shorts being worn by the tank crewman directing his driver; these were heartily detested, and did not survive long in their original form. / *IWM*

Above: Most significant of the reinforcements were the 50 Matilda Infantry Tanks of 7th Royal Tank Regiment. Wavell did not intend to commit these at once, preferring to employ them en masse at a later date against the Italian positions at Sidi Barrani. The Matilda was the most powerful weapon in the British tank armoury, and it was obviously not desirable that the enemy should have any prior warning of its relative invulnerability. / *IWM*

Right: Part of the 7th Royal Tank Regiment, upon which so much of the success in the forthcoming operations would depend. The regiment had fought at Arras in May 1940, where for a time Rommel had personally been under fire from its guns. During Operation Compass and for some months afterwards the Seventh were commanded by Lt-Col R. M. Jerram, son of Vice-Admiral Sir Martyn Jerram who, during World War I, had commanded the China Squadron which pursued von Spee out of the Pacific, and later the 2nd Battle Squadron at Jutland. Poor eyesight had prevented Jerram following his father into the Royal Navy, but after serving in the infantry he had transferred to the Tank Corps in 1917 and the following year had commanded a section of Mark Vs during the assault on the Hindenburg Line. Between the wars he served in Northern Ireland and India, and had been employed on the Staff in France prior to the Dunkirk evacuation. The Seventh's three squadrons were designated A, B and D, the original C Company having been wiped out in World War I, and the regiment's tanks all carried names beginning with G, the seventh letter of the alphabet. / *IWM*

Above: 7 RTR were trained and equipped for the infantry support role. In 1940 this meant that the first wave of Matildas arrived on the objective some 20 minutes ahead of the infantry, the second wave arriving just before bayonets were actually crossed. Once inside the objective the tanks subdued pre-designated areas, particularly machine gun posts, many of which might still be under fire from 'friendly' artillery. The majority of targets would be engaged with the Besa machine gun, but the 2-pdr, which at this stage fired only armour-piercing shot, might be used against buildings and bunker fire slits, and of course the tanks were themselves quite capable of smashing through walls and crushing trenches. If the enemy armour intervened the Matildas would stop whatever they were doing and fight together as tank squadrons. Whilst maintaining their internal integrity, Matilda units operated under the direct command of the infantry formation they were supporting and, after a successful attack, might be required to stand by in case the enemy attempted to retake the lost ground. / *RAC Tank Museum*

Below: 'The country is flat, but not as flat as it looks. It consists of a coastal strip bounded by a series of escarpments of varying height and degree of precipitousness, most of which eventually run into the sea. The coastal strip is bounded either by high cliffs and deep rocky wadis or by sand hills and salt marshes which stop direct access to the sea, except at certain places. The ground is mostly covered with low scrub which grows in isolated roots and gives the impression of acres and acres of enormous, prickly poached eggs. There are many areas where limestone out-crops, boulders and stones predominate, and there is no scrub. The only landmarks are Birs, which are mounds, about the size of a house, of spoil from underground rock cisterns. Most of the Birs are marked on the map, but they are so exactly alike that if used for direction finding they are almost as likely to hinder as to help. There is usually a single fig tree every fifty miles or so and each one is marked on the map with a long name and letters about the same size as Birmingham.' Lt-Col R. M. Jerram, 7 RTR, describing the country over which Operation Compass would be fought. / *Australian War Memorial*

Bottom: During November 7 RTR began training with 4th Indian Division for the attack on the Italian positions south of Sidi Barrani. Only a few staff officers, brigade commanders and the commanders of certain corps troops, 7 RTR included, knew the real purpose of the training, which was carried out under strict security conditions. The soldiers taking part had been told that the manoeuvres, described as Exercise No 1, were simply a rehearsal for a larger corps exercise, to be known as Exercise No 2. Not until the night before the attack itself were they told that Exercise No 2 was Operation Compass.

During the training period, dummy camps representing the Italian positions were laid out from aerial reconnaissance photographs and patrol reports, and 7 RTR practised their penetration techniques with the infantry with whom they were to work. The photograph shows a Matilda troop at the end of a training session, together with the dummy camp and the craters made by the token barrage. / *IWM*

Right: The long approach march from the corps assembly area began on 3 December for the slow Matildas, and on 7 December for 7th Armoured and 4th Indian Divisions. The journey was made in easy stages, with halts for maintenance, and by the night of 8/9 December all units were leaguered in the Enba Gap, poised and ready to strike, the noise of tank tracks and engines being masked by aircraft flying low over the enemy camps.

It was said in the Army that movement orders were not a great deal of use, as 'The Cavalry never read them, the Gunners make their own arrangements, and the Infantry can't understand them.' In this instance, the most meticulous planning had ensured that everyone had arrived in the right place at exactly the right time. Although the whole desert was covered with tanks, guns and vehicles of all types, all moving westward, the Italian Air Force remained out of sight and the movement remained undetected. / *IWM*

Below: Shortly after 0700hrs the whole of 4th Indian Division's artillery, supplemented by the corps' medium and heavy batteries, a total of over 200 guns, opened fire on Nibeiwa. The camp had already been shot up from the east during the night, and for the garrison, already on edge, the bombardment was a shattering start to the day. / *IWM*

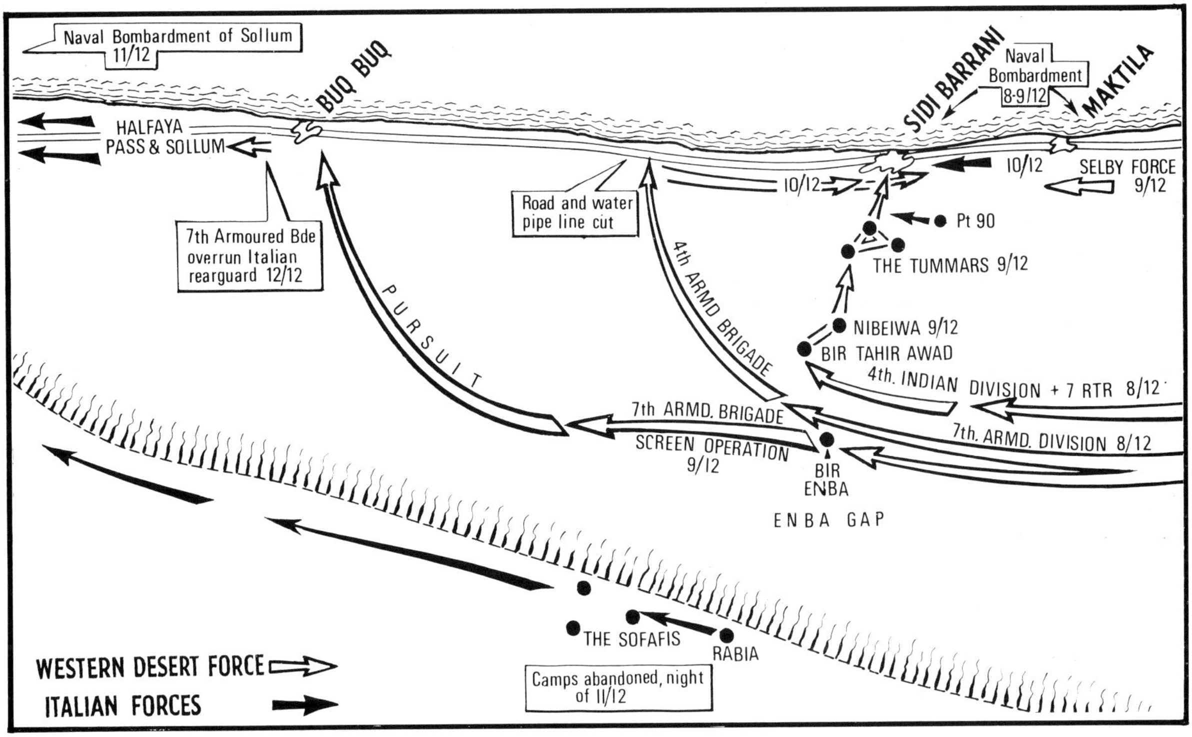

Above: Operation Compass, 8/12 December 1940.

Below: The camp was also combed by the sustained fire of Vickers medium machine guns, making any movement above ground extremely hazardous. The Vickers was a recoil gas-assisted, water cooled weapon with a rate of fire of 450rpm, although a lower rate was used when the gun was employed in the sustained fire role. The water in the cooling jacket boiled after 600 rounds continuous firing, the steam being led off by hose to a condenser can, whence it could be used again on cooling. The gun was very suitable for use in indirect fire on distant reverse slopes and suspected enemy concentrations and, using streamlined ammunition, could engage targets up to 4,500yd away. The Vickers gave good service to the British Army in both world wars, and was not withdrawn until the 1960s. / *IWM*

Right: Meanwhile, far out in the Enba Gap, 4th Armoured Brigade was advancing north to cut the road west of Sidi Barrani, while 7th Armoured Brigade was screening 4th Indian Division's operations against interference from Rabia and the Sofafi chain of camps. At this stage the thunder of the artillery bombardment was rolling across the desert and all eyes were turned towards Nibeiwa where, at 0715hrs on 9 December, the 7th Royal Tank Regiment crossed the start line with A Squadron, commanded by Maj Henry Rew, leading. The formation adopted by Rew was known as 'three up', with three troops each of three tanks in the first wave, as shown here, and the fourth troop and SHQ tanks in the second. Aerial reconnaissance had shown that Nibeiwa was surrounded by an anti-tank ditch, and several tanks had small fascines slung alongside their turrets with which a causeway over this obstacle could be formed; in the event the ditch was too shallow to hinder the Matildas' progress. Behind A Squadron came Col Jerram's Light RHQ tanks, followed at a distance by B Squadron, leading the tracked carriers of the assaulting infantry battalions, 2nd Queen's Own Cameron Highlanders and 1st/6th Rajputana Rifles, the men of which were already jumping from their lorries to form up. Jerram left his D Squadron in reserve near the start line, where the crews had a grandstand view of the whole battle. / *IWM*

Above: Aerial reconnaissance had revealed that the only unmined approach to Nibeiwa was blocked by 23 Italian M11/39 medium tanks. The M11 was a badly designed vehicle, having its 37mm main armament mounted in the front plate of the fighting compartment, giving very little traverse, while the maximum armour thickness was only 29mm. Perhaps even more culpable is the fact that even as 11th Indian Infantry Brigade, spearheaded by 7 RTR's Matildas, bore down on the camp from the west, the crews were only just emerging from their blankets, having apparently been roused by the preliminary bombardment. They were shot down while scrambling aboard their vehicles, not one of which succeeded in moving, and within minutes the tanks themselves had been knocked out by A Squadron, which then carried on to assault the camp itself. One Matilda commander is known to have kicked his gunner repeatedly for missing at point-blank range, when the armour piercing shot was in fact going straight through. This picture of the scene of the engagement was taken the same morning, after the battlefield had been cleaned up. It shows 7 RTR crewmen examining their victims. For the curious there were unpleasant surprises; one Seventh driver, opening the side hatch of a burned out M11, discovered an Italian tank helmet. It contained a charred head.

These M11s were almost the only medium tanks the Italians possessed in the forward area, and represented the operational strength of 2nd Battalion 4th Tank Regiment. The vehicle was prone to mechanical failure, so much so that the regiment's 1st Battalion was refitting in Tobruk, although 70 M11s were theoretically available. / *IWM*

Above: Nibeiwa camp formed an approximate rectangle measuring rather less than 2,500 by 2,000yd, and was held by a division sized formation known as Gruppo Maletti after its commander. The perimeter was ringed by machine gun posts and artillery positions constructed from dry stone breastworks, like the one shown. The scrape in the foreground could well be the 'anti-tank ditch' revealed on the air recce photos, as its depth could easily be exaggerated by morning or evening shadows. The Italian gunners, who had just witnessed the slaughter of their armour, fought their guns to the very muzzle, hitting the advancing Matildas again and again at point-blank range without visible result. Many clambered on to their sangar walls to shoot or throw grenades at the lumbering tanks until they were shot down by the chattering Besas, while their comrades died around the guns they served to the bitter end. Throughout the campaign they showed the same self-sacrificial courage, earning the unstinted praise of friend and foe, and were the best element of their Army. Once their artillery had been silenced, the Italian infantry tended to lose heart. / *IWM*

Below: Some of the 4,000 prisoners taken at Nibeiwa. To quote the history of the 4th Indian Division: 'Frightened, dazed or desperate Italians erupted from tents and slit trenches, some to surrender supinely, others to leap gallantly into battle, hurling grenades or blazing machine guns in futile belabour of the impregnable intruders . . . General Maletti, the Italian commander, sprang from his dug-out, machine gun in hand. He fell from an answering burst; his son beside him was struck down and captured.' Nonetheless, fighting continued for another two and a half hours, and as one Matilda crewman put it, 'The Italians may have been a push-over afterwards, but they fought like hell at Nibeiwa.' / *IWM*

Below: The Seventh's casualties at Nibeiwa consisted of two killed and six wounded. Maj Rew was killed when he opened his cupola at the height of the action, and four more casualties occurred in one tank when the driver slid back his visor and received a burst from this 20mm anti-aircraft gun. He too was killed and every man in the turret crew wounded as the rounds richocheted round inside. The strain on the medical services, both British and Italian, was enormous, and it was many hours before the tank's loader/operator could be evacuated. He had lost a part of his foot, and by then the wound had turned gangrenous, so that the jolting of the ambulance over the desert produced waves of unendurable agony, causing him to writhe uncontrollably. Only the constant attention of the wounded Italians who shared the ambulance prevented him from sustaining further injury. These men owed the Matilda crews nothing, but it was thanks to their humanity that he survived. / *IWM*

Bottom: With Cromwellian thoroughness, Jerram hammered into his regiment the fact that the Forward Rally after a successful attack was the place where the next attack was won. Once released by the infantry the tanks returned at once to the rally point, which had been fixed beforehand, and received immediate replenishment of petrol, oil and ammunition. This was the place where damaged track links could be replaced and minor repairs put in hand. After their first actions the Seventh's fitters always brought their oxy-acetylene cutting torches to the rally point so that they could free turrets jammed by shell fragments fused against the turret ring. The photograph, taken during the Sidi Barrani battles, shows a typical rally point. / *IWM*

Left: Once it was clear that Nibeiwa had fallen Jerram set off for the next objective, Tummar West, followed by his Matildas and 5th Indian Infantry Brigade, who were to carry out the attack. Meanwhile the artillery limbered up to move to new fire positions. A sudden sandstorm made the location of the camp difficult, and the assault centre line was chosen by compass, this calculated risk proving entirely justified. The Seventh went in with D Squadron leading, supported by a composite squadron, a total of 22 tanks. Once again the enemy gunners fought courageously until shot down, but the regiment experienced no difficulty in breaking into the camp and suffered only four men slightly wounded. / *IWM*

Above centre: At Tummar West Gen Piscatori's 2nd Libyan Division fought ferociously in defence of every trench and dug-out, and it took two hours' hard fighting with bayonet and grenade before 1st Royal Fusiliers and 3rd/1st Punjabis could subdue the position, which yielded 2,000 prisoners. The British battalion had been driven to within 150 yards of the camp's perimeter by New Zealand Service Corps drivers, who then snatched their rifles and went into the assault with the Fusiliers. When the fighting ended, Jerram was horrified to learn that the commander of 5th Indian Infantry Brigade intended keeping 15 of his precious Matildas as a safeguard against counter-attack. Nine tanks had already been left at Nibeiwa for the same purpose, and as the regiment also had a number of vehicles temporarily out of action with track damage caused by mines and gunfire, this decision reduced the effective strength of 7 RTR to a mere seven tanks with which to tackle the camps of Trummar Central and East. / *IWM*

Above: The tanks rallied at Inaba, a mud hut north of Tummar West, at about 1500hrs, and were joined shortly afterwards by two repaired mine casualties which arrived from Nibeiwa. Two turrets were jammed by shell splinters, but Jerram decided to commit the tanks for their moral effect, and formed a composite squadron of three troops under Captain Badrock which left for Tummar East at 1555hrs in the wake of the artillery and 4th/6th Rajputanas. En route one of Badrock's troops went slightly off course and received the surrender of the smaller camp of Tummar Central which contained a large number of demoralised fugitives from Nibeiwa and Tummar West, who had communicated their own terror of the Matildas to the occupants. At Tummar East the position was the same and the task rendered even easier by a large part of the garrison having been defeated with much slaughter in the open while attempting to counter-attack Tummar West. By the end of the day 7 RTR had carried out four successful attacks, and although everyone was tired and hungry, having eaten nothing more than a few hard-tack biscuits during the past 24 hours, the regiment was, in Jerram's words, 'On top of the world.' / *IWM*

Left: During the afternoon of 9 December the Reggia Aeronautica attempted to intervene in the battle. It was an impossible task, since the RAF were present in strength over the combat zone.

This SM79 bomber was damaged by fire from a Hurricane and crash landed on an airstrip near Sidi Barrani with three of its crew dead. The survivors were made prisoner immediately, as the airstrip was already in British hands. The Savoia-Marchetti SM79 Sparviero (Hawk) was a robust and reliable medium bomber. Capable of 270mph, it carried a 2,200lb bomb load and was armed with three 12.7mm machine guns, supplemented by one 7.7mm machine gun which could be fired from the beam windows. The open dorsal gun position and directional aerial can clearly be seen. The SM79s were manned by a crew of five and powered by three Piaggio 1,000hp engines. / *IWM*

Centre right: By the morning of 10 December Jerram could produce a composite squadron of eight tanks and set off north to locate 16th British Brigade, which had been detailed to assault Sidi Barrani from the west. Unfortunately the Brigade was subjected to heavy shelling while leaving its lorries, and was not in a position to attack when the Matildas arrived. To ease the pressure on the infantry Jerram decided to suppress the Italian artillery alone, and carried out a 4,000yd advance into the heart of the enemy batteries, destroying seven in an hour's close fighting before returning with 200 prisoners. During the Seventh's attack the regiment was also under fire from British artillery engaging the Sidi Barrani defences, which was unavoidable in the circumstances, although the arrival of the 60-pdr shells in particular was a matter of some concern. Two tanks broke through to the shore, where one, *Gitana*, had a track shot away. After they had shot off their ammunition the crew surrended, setting fire to the tank, but succeeded in persuading their captors to surrender in turn, later in the day. *Gitana* was the only Matilda lost by enemy action during the entire offensive. The photograph shows the Seventh's leading wave coming under fire as they approach the Sidi Barrani perimeter. / *IWM*

Bottom right: Sidi Barrani contained the headquarters of General Gallina, commander of the Libyan Group. On 9 December Gallina had signalled Graziani that the desert to the south was crawling with British armour against which he had no defence, and that he had lost contact with his 2nd Libyan Division. The same day his water supply pipeline and communications to the west were severed by 4th Armoured Brigade.

Already savaged by the Matildas' morning attack, the Blackshirt garrison was in no mood for prolonged resistance when the reorganised assault was resumed at 1600hrs on the 10th. While 2 RTR attacked the western defences, 7 RTR supported the infantry on to their objectives and 6 RTR moved round the eastern perimeter to intercept 1st Libyan Division, which was withdrawing from its advanced position at Maktila.

Once the Sidi Barrani defences had been breached again, resistance collapsed almost at once, but 6 RTR found that the Libyans to the east were still full of fight, although cut off and surrounded, and did not receive their surrender until the following morning. / *IWM*

Above: An element of the deception plan for Operation Compass involved part of the Mersa Matruh garrison, known as Selby Force, mounting a diversionary attack on Maktila while it was bombarded from the sea. On the morning of 10 December it was discovered that 1st Libyan Division had gone, and Selby Force could only give chase. Some of the Libyans managed to avoid the trap set by 6 RTR on the coast road, for during the night a convoy of 45 10-ton lorries drove straight into Sidi Barrani from the east, under the impression that it was still in Italian hands. They were snapped up at once, and 7 RTR managed to retain six of these useful vehicles, which eased the regiment's transport problems considerably.

On 11 December nine Matildas were despatched to Point 90, the last enemy camp in the area, and succeeded in occupying it without incident. That night the Italians evacuated their camps at Rabia and Sofafi and slipped away towards the frontier under cover of a sand storm.

The photograph shows one of the Seventh's Matildas leaving Sidi Barrani for the regimental concentration area at Bir Tahir Awad, from which point it had been intended to launch attacks on the now abandoned camps on 12 December. / *IWM*

Below: With the fall of Sidi Barrani the original aim of Operation Compass had been achieved, and on the night of 10/11 December Wavell removed 4th Indian Division from O'Connor's command for transfer to the Sudan front. This left O'Connor with only 7th Armoured Division and 16th British Brigade to continue the pursuit, for although he was promised 6th Australian Division as a replacement it would be some time before this formation could complete its move to the front from Palestine. To commemorate their arrival in Sidi Barrani, the Italians had erected a suitable monument, and vehicles of 4th Royal Horse Artillery are seen driving past this as they move west in support of the armoured brigades. The towed gun is a 25-pdr. / *IWM*

Left: The Matilda's massive 80mm frontal casting, invulnverable to every Italian tank, anti-tank and field gun. The fighting at Nibeiwa, the Tummars and Sidi Barrani proved that the tank was almost impossible to stop, was agile enough to batter its way through or crawl over most field defences, and could deal with the enemy armour with almost total immunity. In spite of the small numbers employed later in the campaign, word of these qualities had spread like wildfire through the Italian Army, and the Matilda was regarded as a terror weapon against which there was no adequate defence. The point was fully appreciated by one crew. / *IWM*

Right: Marshal Rodolfo Graziani, Marchese di Noghelli.

The success of the Sidi Barrani operations threw Graziani completely off balance. After signalling Rome on 11 December that 'four divisions can be considered destroyed', he followed this the next day by announcing that he was seriously considering a withdrawal to Tripoli (sic), 'in order to keep the flag flying over that fortress at least', and complaining that he was compelled to wage 'the war of the flea against the elephant.' In the midst of his mood of black despair he wrote to his wife, enclosing his will and commenting that 'one cannot break steel armour with finger nails alone.'

Mussolini refused to believe that the news could possibly be as bad as Graziani suggested, and passed scathing judgement upon his Commander-in-Chief in North Africa: 'This man has lost his mind or at least his senses. Here is another man with whom I cannot get angry, because I despise him.' / *Radio Times Hulton Picture Library*

Above: Knocked out light tanks of 3rd King's Own Hussars on the salt flats west of Buq Buq.

12 December found 7th Armoured Brigade wheeling in towards the coast to cut off the retreating enemy. Unfortunately the wheel was completed too late, and by the time the leading regiment, 3rd Hussars, had reached the coast road, the Italians had gone.

3rd Hussars set off in pursuit of the enemy rearguard, which was located lining a semi-circle of sand dunes behind a salt marsh, its massed artillery covering the route westwards. The crust of a salt flat can be many feet thick, or it can be paper thin. In this instance the comparatively inexperienced 3rd Hussars were unlucky, and their attempt to close the range by a headlong attack across the flats was stalled as their tanks broke through the crust and wallowed to a stand-still among the bursting shells / *IWM*

Below: The effect of a direct hit upon a Light Mark VI.

Within minutes the leading squadron had been shot to pieces.

It was 7th Armoured Division's policy that each regiment should have at least one cruiser squadron, and 3rd Hussars had exchanged its B Squadron complete for that of 2 RTR. The Second's cruisers had not been committed to the attack, and their crews could only look on in horror as the Third's light tanks were battered to destruction. Arnold Jackson, 20-year old auxiliary turret gunner in an A9, saw a man with whom he had been talking only hours earlier, cut in two by a Breda machine gun as he staggered away from his blazing tank. A second later the turret was blown out of another Light; the return fire of the tanks was taking some toll of the Italian gun crews, but Jackson's impression was that reserve crews were standing by, and that they were only too ready and willing to continue the fight. / *IWM*

Left: Next to arrive on the scene were the 8th King's Royal Irish Hussars, who manoeuvred their tanks on to the flank of the enemy position while a battery of 4th RHA shelled the objective with their 25-pdrs. The 8th Hussars' regimental historian (*Men of valour*: Olivia Fitzroy) describes the ensuing action:
'C Squadron came round either side of the hills guns blazing. SHQ and the cruiser tanks in the centre and the Mark VIs on either flank. The Italians opened up and the guns, which until recently had been facing west and firing on 3rd Hussars, were brought hastily to bear on C Squadron.

'However, an action that looked like developing into a second Balaclava, soon stopped. Nelson in a cruiser hit a lorry which was drawn up behind the gun line with his third shot. This proved to be full of ammunition and blew up with the most terrifying crash. It was all too much for the Italians, and before they had recovered C Squadron was into the gun line.'
B Squadron 2 RTR had also spotted a way forward and were storming their way into the Italian position. / *IWM*

Right: Looking north-west from the south-east corner of the Italian position at Buq Buq. This is the area in which B Squadron 2 RTR entered the defences, and one of the guns has been swung round to deal with the threat; possibly this is the weapon which knocked out the tank of the squadron's second-in-command, Capt Duncan. Although the area was crawling with machine gun posts, Duncan and his driver, Cpl Cox, scrambled from their vehicle and attacked the Italians with their pistols, obtaining their surrender almost at once. / *IWM*

Centre right: A view from further round the position, which clearly indicates that the Italians intended to make a determined stand. On the far right is one of 3rd Hussars' light tanks, knocked out on the salt flat. / *IWM*

Bottom right: Prisoners beginning to assemble on the Buq Buq battlefield. Asked to supply an estimate of the number of men captured, a Hussar officer found himself in difficulties, as more and more captives were rounded up and brought in from the west. A head count was impossible, but the Hussar was able to gauge the amount of land occupied by the growing throng, and was able to transmit, 'So far as I can see, there are twenty acres of officers and a hundred acres of men!' It was sufficient for the moment. In fact 14,000 men and 68 guns were captured at Buq Buq. The tanks belong to B Squadron 2 RTR. / *IWM*

Top: So far, Operation Compass and its sequel had yielded 38,000 prisoners, including four generals, 237 guns and 73 light and medium tanks. Group Maletti, 1st and 2nd Libyan Divisions and 4th Blackshirt Division had ceased to exist, and the remaining Italian units in Egypt were running hard for the frontier. The prisoners outnumbered the entire garrison of Egypt, let alone the reduced Western Desert Force, which was hard put to supply its captives with drinking water.

Long columns of docile men could be found being shepherded to the east by single British infantrymen, while elsewhere Italians organised convoys with their own trucks and ran an unescorted shuttle service to the prisoner of war compounds. Had they not cooperated to this extent it is probable that many Italians would have died of hunger or thirst, for the British could not have foreseen the sheer scale of the problem and were simply not equipped to feed so many extra mouths in the field. / *IWM*

Above: Officers of the 3rd Hussars. Left, Cap T. Somerville, RAMC, Medical Officer; centre, Lt-Col W. G. Petherick, Commanding Officer; right, Maj A. Dawes, Adjutant. Somerville was awarded the DSO for attending the wounded under fire at Buq Buq; he later died in the mountains of Crete, trying to avoid capture. Dawes was killed at El Alamein. The 'Galloping Third' was noted for its dash, but suffered heavy casualties amongst its officers. The light tank in the background is flying a full set of pennons for C Squadron Leader, whose operator is on wireless watch; a collapsible table and an Italian helmet, used as a washbasin, provide some elementary comfort. / *IWM*

Left: Two days after Buq Buq, the 3rd Hussars reached Fort Capuzzo and captured an officer and 30 men, who surrendered to this solitary light tank. By now most of the Italians who were still free had crossed the frontier and had entered the fortress of Bardia. A squadron of 1 RTR which tried to effect a pentration by coup de main lost one tank and had several others damaged, and it was now obvious that Bardia could only be reduced by formal siege.

To the south the Italians were still holding Sidi Omar, which they had fortified in the manner of the Sidi Barrani camps. 4th Armoured Brigade attacked the position on 16 December and, after an artillery bombardment, 7th Hussars and 2 RTR charged into the defences. Capt P. R. C. Hobart, commanding the Second's C Squadron, smashed his way into the main fort in an A9, losing his front idler wheel in the process, and with the arrival of a second tank inside the walls the defenders' resolve cracked. Sidi Omar yielded a further 900 prisoners and several guns, its fall signalling the complete domination of the Frontier Zone by 7th Armoured Division. / *IWM*

Below: After the Sidi Barnani battles, 7 RTR were able to concentrate their tanks for the first time for several days and carry out some heavy maintenance, in which a large machinery truck captured a Nibeiwa proved to be of invaluable assiatance. The long approach march and two days fighting had taken its toll of the Matildas' steering clutches, the linings of which wore out very rapidly. Further wear was to be avoided if at all possible, and in their move up the frontier the tanks had the assistance of Scammel gun tractors to ease them round the hairpin bends of the Halfaya Pass although, as the picture shows, they made the climb under their own power. In the background is the Gulf of Sollum, with the upper and lower towns seen on the left. / *IWM*

Bardia to Derna

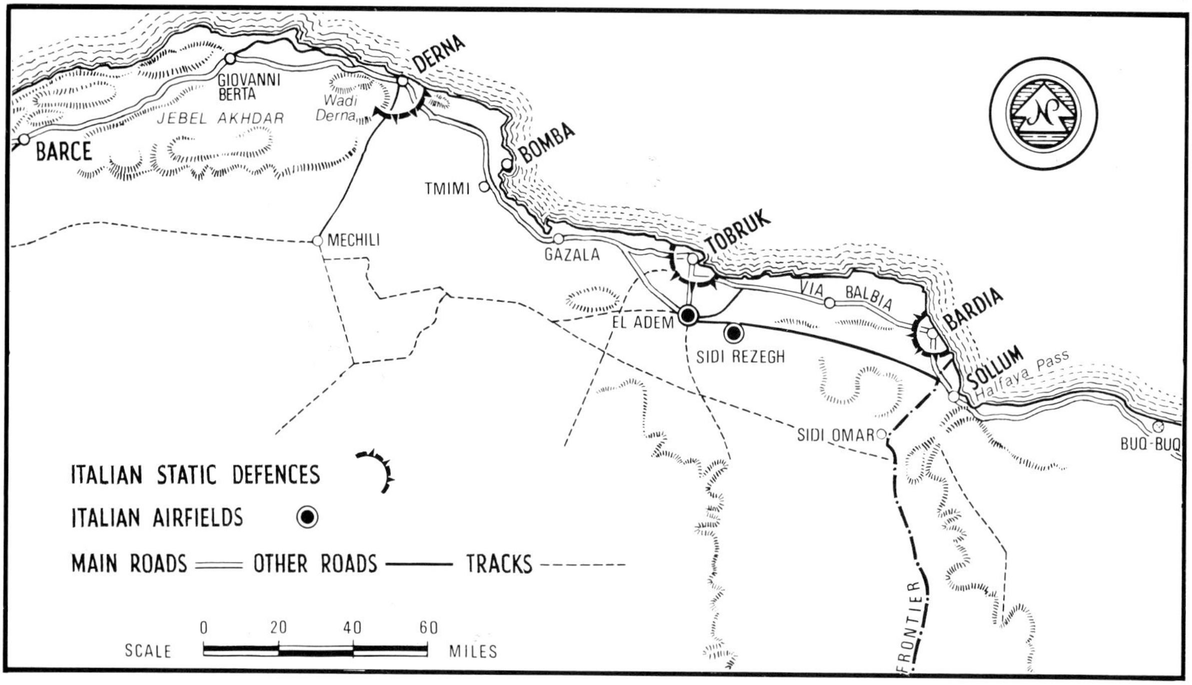

Above: Bardia to Derna. Officially, Operation Compass ended with the destruction of the Italian forces in Egypt and along the frontier, but Wavell had no hestitation in reinforcing O'Connor's success by permitting him to advance into enemy territory. The arrival of 6th Australian Division enabled XIII Corps, as the Western Desert Force became known on 1 January, to assault Bardia and Tobruk and to advance to the last Italian defence line in Cyrenaica, and Wadi Derna, capturing in the process the last of the Reggia Aeronautica's forward airfields.

Below: Christmas Day dawned cold and largely comfortless for the majority of Western Desert Force, but for some crews, like that of this Light Mark VI, it provided an opportunity to broach their store of preciously hoarded 'goodies'. Beer and tinned salmon may seem a strange way to breakfast, but such things were an unimaginable delicacy, and must have been looked forward to with relish. In this picture there is evidence of desert sores, cuts and abrasions which refused to heal because of the prevailing conditions. */ IWM*

Left: After the disasters in Egypt, Mussolini had high hopes that a successful defence of Bardia would do much to restore the situation in North Africa. It seemed unlikely that the fortress, garrisoned by 45,000 men supported by 400 guns and over 100 tanks, was in immediate danger, for its defences were much stronger than those of the Sidi Barrani camps, the 17-mile perimeter beng enclosed by a continuous anti-tank ditch behind which lay barbed wire aprons, concrete emplacements and block houses with interlocking arcs of fire. To its commander, Gen Bergonzoli, an officer with a dramatically forked beard, the Duce sent a personal message, expressing confidence that 'Electric Beard and his brave soldiers will stand at whatever cost, faithful to the last.' The message was tactless in the extreme, for not only did it do nothing to bolster Bergonzoli's already shaky confidence, it also provided O'Connor's men with an apparent figure of fun for an enemy, to be known thereafter as 'Electric Whiskers'.

Mussolini's experience of mountain warfare during World War I made the defeat of his armies in Greece at least intelligible to him, but he was unable to grasp the nature of the war which was being forced on his generals in North Africa. / *Radio Times Hulton Picture Library*

Below: Following the Sidi Barrani battles, Maj-Gen O'Moore Creagh visited 7 RTR and discussed with Jerram the suitability of 7th Armoured Division's cruisers for the infantry support role. Jerram showed him the dented and gashed armour of his Matildas, pointing out one tank which had already sustained no less than 40 major hits, and Creagh abandoned the idea. These examples of battle damage, seen shortly after 7 RTR had returned to Egypt for a refit, may be taken as typical. Although the Italians had the capacity to sever tracks and jam turret rings, they were never able to penetrate the Matilda's main armour. / *IWM*

Left: For the coming assault on Bardia 7 RTR was able to field a total of five troops organised as a composite squadron. Maj-Gen Mackay, whose 6th Australian Division would be making the assault with the support of the Seventh, was in no doubt about the value of the Matildas, each one 'being worth a battalion of infantry' to him. He placed half his divisional workshops at Jerram's disposal, and gave instructions that no efforts were to be spared to get damaged tanks back into the fight. During the fighting several of the Seventh's non-runners were towed out to the edge of captured ground to act as anti-tank and machine gun posts. The Matilda's combat efficiency was to some extent purchased at the expense of a heavy maintenance work-load for its crew. This particular crew are about to embark on the interminable task of servicing the vehicle's numerous grease nipples; the heat of the day seems to have softened the grease sufficiently for it to be poured directly into the grease gun, a very minor compensation for service in such harsh conditions! / *IWM*

Centre right: Having selected a suitable point to break into the Bardia defences, the Royal Australian Engineers constructed a full scale replica, including the anti-tank ditch, dummy mine fields and wire entanglements. During the subsequent rehearsals for the attack a suitable battle drill was worked out in conjunction with the assault infantry and the Matildas.

An hour before dawn on 3 January an Australian infantry battalion rushed three enemy posts across the ditch, closely followed by three parties of engineers; one to clear a path through the mines, another to cut the wire with Bangalore torpedoes, and the third to construct six crossing places for the tanks by throwing down the sides of the ditch and constructing causeways with the materials. This photograph shows a section of the ditch and one of the tank causeways, to the left of which can be seen the shaded lantern marking its position. The first two troops of Matildas began to cross at 0640hrs, and turned respectively left and right, rolling up the Italian posts along the perimeter, each followed by an infantry battalion which mopped up in their wake. The second two troops also followed this procedure, but struck deeper into the defences, creating an ever widening circle. In the distance can be seen something of the artillery bombardment. / *IWM*

Bottom right: The morning dawned cold and misty and the Australians were ordered to don battle order over their greatcoats. In the background sappers are constructing further causeways across the ditch and beginning to deal with the wire while the infantrymen wait to move forward. / *IWM*

Above: A troop of 25-pdrs in action against Bardia. The fixed defences and known gun positions were hammered by the corps and divisional artillery both before and during the assault. Limbers drawn up alongside the guns and spare ammunition boxes indicate a prolonged fire-support programme. The gun line has been slightly staggered as a defence against air attack. The gun nearest the camera has just fired and its barrel is in full recoil. The range of the 25-pdr was 13,500yd, over 3,000yd more than that of its Italian counterpart, the 100/17, although the latter's weight of shell was greater at 30lb. / *IWM*

Below: Some of the British medium and heavy artillery dated from World War I, although the weapons themselves had been fitted to modern carriages. The use of 60-pdr guns at Sidi Barrani has already been mentioned, but there were also a number of 6-inch howitzers available, one of which is seen being manhandled into its firing position in front of Bardia. The 6-inch howitzer threw an 86lb shell 11,400yd. / *IWM*

Above: To add to the discomfiture of the defenders the battleships *Barham, Valiant* and *Warspite* pounded specific targets within the perimeter with salvo after salvo from their 15-inch guns. Those who have survived a naval bombardment bear witness to the shattering nature of the experience, which can leave normal, well balanced men speechless for several hours after the event. Crouched within their dug-outs, the Italians must have reflected bitterly on the incapacity of their own Navy to prevent the incessant forays by British warships against their seaward flank.

Before the year was out they had some measure of revenge. On 25 November *Barham* was torpedoed by *U331* some 60 miles north of Sollum, and sank with heavy loss of life. During the night of 18/19 December Italian human torpedoes severely damaged *Valiant* in Alexandria harbour. All three ships belonged to the Queen Elizabeth class, and each mounted eight 15-inch guns. They had served together in the 5th Battle Squadron at Jutland. *Warspite* survived World War II, as did *Valiant*, and escaped the indignity of the breaker's yard by running herself on to the rocks of Prussia Cove during what was to be her final voyage. / *IWM*

Above: The fighting within the perimeter is vividly described in the Australian history of the campaign, *To Benghazi:*
'In the first few posts, the Italians fought it out, their tracer shells striking the heavy armour of the tanks and ricocheting high in the air. Some garrisons surrendered after the tanks, blazing with 2-pounders and machine guns, had circled them, but generally there was a sharp little battle, sometimes for a quarter of an hour. Two or three of the cumbrous tanks would concentrate their fire on one post, whilst a platoon fired with rifle and bren from close behind. When the Italian fire seemed to have been subdued, the infantrymen moved forward, sometimes cautiously, sometimes with a rush, and threw grenades into the concrete sided gun pits.' By late afternoon the defences had been all but cut in two, and men were coming forward in large numbers to surrender. The attack was resumed the following morning, and by 1600hrs the port itself was in Australian hands. / *IWM*

Below: A typical Italian dug-out in Bardia, no doubt the living accommodation of the crew of this abandoned anti-aircraft gun. / *IWM*

Top: On the southern sector, the attack of 17th Australian Infantry Brigade had not been supported by armour, and the Italians had been able to hold their own. With the collapse of resistance elsewhere, Jerram was able to despatch two troops of Matildas on the morning of 5 January, and their influence proved to be decisive. By 1700hrs the Italians had laid down their arms. Total British and Australian casualties incurred during the capture of Bardia amounted to 500, of whom only 150 were killed; 7 RTR's casualties were two killed and four wounded. / *IWM*

Above: The following day Mackay set his division in motion towards Tobruk, some 70 miles distant to the west. Here, 7 RTR are seen moving along the Via Balbia, their tanks maintaining the mandatory half-speed imposed by Jerram when they were out of contact with the enemy. Although already deeply immersed in the details of the next operation, O'Connor found time to write Jerram a personal note concerning the regiment's performance at Bardia, commenting: 'It has been a wonderful show, and you are more than ever responsible for its success.' / *Australian War Memorial*

Above: **The massive Italian surrenders and the discovery of field bordellos, 'enamelled baths, silken garments and cosmetics' in numerous dug-outs provoked the contempt of the battle grimed and weary Australian infantrymen. As always, the Italian Staff officers presented themselves with dressed hair and polished boots, their smart appearance a marked contrast with that of their men. Groups such as this can have done little to alter Australian opinions.** / *IWM*

Below: **A total of 38,000 men began the long trudge from Bardia towards the Egyptian frontier, whence, by degrees, they were transported to the already bursting prisoner of war cages in the Nile Delta. As the photograph shows, the tiny escort could have been easily swamped if any of the prisoners had wanted to escape, but their expressions clearly indicate that they have had enough, and demoralisation is complete. 'Electric Whiskers' Bergonzoli was not among the prisoners; he successfully evaded capture and made his way to Tobruk.** / *IWM*

Above: **In terms of booty, Bardia yielded over 700 assorted vehicles many in working order. These might have eased many of XII Corps' logistic problems, but the difficulty was finding sufficient drivers to man them. Some units employed Italian drivers, but the practice was frowned upon and eventually forbidden. XII Corps also captured 120 tanks, mostly of the light CV type seen here being examined by a despatch rider on a road above the harbour. The vehicle on the left seems to be an early model mounting a single 6.5mm air-cooled Fiat Type 14 machine gun, while that on the right carries the more conventional twin 8mm Breda machine guns. A half-hearted attempt has been made to increase the scant protection of the 12mm armour by piling a few rocks on to the glacis plate. Italian armour played little part in the battle for the fortress.** */ IWM*

Right: **The numbers of small arms captured remained an unknown quantity. There was neither the time nor the manpower available to count the piles of abandoned weapons.** */ IWM*

Top: Some of the 400 guns surrendered at Bardia. In the foreground and on the left are examples of the 104/40 medium gun, in the centre a line of 100mm 100/17 field howitzers, and on the right a battery of 75mm field guns. / *IWM*

Above: Several of the guns taken deserved a place in a museum. One might be forgiven for imagining that these ancient fortress muzzle loaders had been deployed solely to draw British fire away from more worthwhile targets, but the careful construction of the sangars, allowing sufficient room for the crews to serve their weapons from the front, and the presence of rammer staves, suggests that the guns were expected to play a part in the battle. Only the empty Cinzano bottle seems to belong to the 20th century. / *IWM*

Top right: Throughout the fighting in Bardia, 7th Armoured Division had stood guard against interference from the south and west. Now, its cruisers moved again in the van of XIII Corps to isolate Tobruk. Sheer mechanical attrition was beginning to take its toll of regimental strengths to such an extent that two regiments, 8th Hussars and 6 RTR, were removed from the order of battle, handing over their tanks before returning to Egypt for a refit. / *IWM*

Centre right: The 6th Australian Divisional Cavalry Regiment equipped itself with M11 and M13 medium tanks captured at Bardia, painting them with large white kangaroos to avoid confusion. The regiment declined to follow British practice in lettering its squadrons, calling them instead Ringo, Rabbit and Wombat. Ringo is recorded as having five M11s and one M13, while Rabbit and Wombat each had two M13s. / *IWM*

Left: Few warships can have been as well known and so popular with an army as were the little Insect class gunboats of Force W, later to be known as the Inshore Squadron. The Insects had originally served on the China Station and had a long and eventful history. Their primary armament was two 6-inch guns with a maximum range of 12,000yd, but they also carried several 3-pounders for close action and a variety of anti-aircraft weapons.

As originally constituted, Force W consisted of the *Aphis* and *Ladybird*, joined later by the 15-inch gun monitor *Terror* and a third Insect, *Gnat.* Based on Mersa Matruh, Force W was a constant thorn in the Italians' side. Its ships bombarded them when they advanced into Egypt, and again as they withdrew. They shelled Maktila and Sidi Barrani during Operation Compass; they took part in the fleet bombardment of Bardia; and they engaged targets in Tobruk as XIII Corps stormed its way into the fortress. On the night of 23/24 August *Ladybird* impudently steamed right into Bardia harbour and, finding it empty, shot up everything in sight; on 17 December *Aphis* repeated the performance, sinking three enemy freighters as well.

In addition, the Insects acted as supply carriers, delivering 100 tons of urgently needed drinking water daily for a period, ferried in reinforcements and shipped out prisoners. The photograph was taken in the Gulf of Sollum. / *IWM*

Above: The same meticulous preparation went into the taking of Tobruk as had gone into that of Bardia. 7 RTR produced 18 Matildas for the operation, formed into a composite squadron under Maj K. P. Harris, who is seen here briefing his vehicle commanders. / *IWM*

Below: An identical battle drill was followed, and at 0630hrs on 21 January the perimeter was penetrated. Several hours' hard fighting followed in which the Italians brought their heavy coast defence guns to bear. Ironically, the point of entry was also that chosen by Rommel when he stormed the fortress in June 1942. / *IWM*

Above: Once again, the Italian field artillery distinguished itself. These guns seem to have been dragged from their emplacements and realigned for firing over open sights, almost certainly against Matildas. / *IWM*

Left: But neither direct gunfire nor a variety of obstacles could stop the combination of tanks and Digger infantry. Post after post was stormed or surrendered, until the defence was all but torn in two. In this sort of battle it is unlikely that the extra cans of drinking water stowed on the rear of this Matilda would have lasted very long. / *IWM*

Above right: Throughout the day troops returned to the regimental rally point for replenishment and running battle repairs, to be despatched again to fresh objectives. By nightfall the attackers had reached the edge of the escarpment overlooking the town itself, and the hours of darkness were rent by the thunder of demolitions and pierced by the glow of burning Italian stores. / *IWM*

Right: Resistance the following morning was negligible, and Harris took two composite troops into Tobruk town in support of 19th Australian Infantry Brigade. Many of the garrison had already packed and were ready to leave. / *IWM*

Above: 6th Australian Divisional Cavalry had no intention of being left out in the cold, and penetrated as far as the waterfront. The squadron concerned was almost certainly Ringo, since the tank on the left is an M13, while that on the right is an M11. Severe though the demolitions may appear, there were still sufficient stores left intact to supply XIII Corps with many of its requirements for a continued advance. / *IWM*

Centre right: The brilliant muzzle flash of a 7.2-inch howitzer as it sends its 202lb projectile screaming on its way into the Tobruk defences. This weapon had a range of 16,000yd. / *IWM*

Bottom right: A 6-inch howitzer in action against Tobruk. The detachment commander has just jerked the lanyard and the barrel is running in on recoil. The men's dress may not be up to Larkhill standards, but their gun drill remains immaculate. / *IWM*

Above: Gun flashes and tracer highlight a night bombardment. The Tobruk garrison, consisting of the 61st Division, some 9,000 stragglers from vanished formations, and a naval detachment of 2,000 men, were protected by defences similar to those of Bardia, supported by over 200 guns and 90 tanks. Their orders were to hold to the last, but the fate of Bardia had depressed them, and they could only wait in gloomy resignation for the onslaught of the terrible Matildas and the equally frightening Australian infantry. / *IWM*

Below: Some of the 25,000 prisoners setting out on their long journey east. They left behind them all their artillery and a further 87 tanks. In Fort Solaro the garrison commander, Gen Manella, described as 'an old man, dignified and quiet and very tired', surrendered his pistol to an Australian company commander, insisting that his surrender was a personal matter and did not apply to the troops under his command. Although his soldiers fully appreciated that further resistance was pointless, there was an integrity in Manella's conduct which was absent 17 months later when Gen Klopper pronounced a General Surrender of the British garrison of Tobruk in similar circumstances. / *IWM*

Right: **The grounded, burned-out hulk of the Italian cruiser *San Giorgio* in Tobruk harbour. For a while the cruiser had been able to support the defenders with the fire of her guns.** / *IWM*

Below: **Maj K.P. Harris, commander of 7 RTR's composite squadron at Tobruk, flying a captured flag from his tank. After Tobruk, events moved too quickly for the Matildas to be used again, although eight did reach Mechili. The Seventh was then withdrawn by sea and rail to Alexandria for an extensive refit, its tanks having done an average mileage of 1,200. Commenting on the regiment's achievements, the late Sir Basil Liddell Hart said that: 'The history of war shows no case of a single fighting unit having such a great effect in deciding the issue of battles, and of a campaign. The record of 7 RTR in this campaign is peerless: by any measure and in the strictest sense of the term.'**

Still equipped with Matildas the Seventh fought in most of the subsequent desert battles until involved in the general surrender at Tobruk in June 1942. A new Seventh was raised from 10 RTR, fighting in Normandy with Churchills and later converting to Crocodile flame-throwers, which it later took to Korea. The regiment was disbanded following one of the apparently endless series of defence cuts. / *IWM*

Left: A Cant Z1007bis medium bomber. Until its operational airfields around Tobruk were over run, the Italian bomber force did its best to slow up the British advance, but however persistent its efforts, they were no substitute for organised ground forces. At best the attacks had a nuisance value; at worst they caused injury and loss of life among their own people by the occasional bombing of prisoner of war enclosures. The Z1007 series were also known as the Alcione (Kingfishers) and carried a bomb load of 4,410lb. Their maximum speed was 280mph and operational ceiling 26,500ft. Four machine guns were carried, one each in the beam hatches, the dorsal and ventral turrets. The aircraft was powered by three 1,000hp Piaggio engines. / *IWM*

Right: El Adem, January 1941. Once its complex of tactical airfields around Tobruk had been over run, the Reggia Aeronautica could take little further part in the campaign, since with the exception of the airport at Benghazi the remaining bases near Tripoli were out of range.

The twin engined aircraft is a general purpose Caproni Ca309 Ghibli (Desert Wind). The light tank carries the original 7th Armoured Division tactical sign, a red square enclosing a white circle; the famous jerboa began appearing in the centre of the circle about this time.

The second photograph, taken near Gazala, shows (left) the wreckage of a Fiat CR32 single-seater biplane fighter, an even more obsolescent design than the CR42. The CR32 had flown during the Spanish Civil War and had been widely used for air displays. With a top speed of only 233mph it was the slowest fighter in North Africa, and although it continued in service until 1942, its use was latterly confined to night operations. / *IWM*

Right: Count Galeazzo Ciano, Italian Foreign Minister.

As disaster followed upon disaster, Mussolini obstinately refused to face facts, and radiated a totally unrealistic optimism. As the Italian Army struggled to form a new defensive line based on Derna, Ciano completely lost patience with his father-in-law, and gave vent to an entirely justified outburst of rage: 'At Sidi Barrani, they spoke of surprise. Then, you counted upon Bardia, where Bergonzoli was, the heroic Bergonzoli. Bardia yielded after two hours. Then you placed your hopes on Tobruk because Pitassi Mannella, the King of Artillerymen, was there. Now, you speak with great faith of the escarpment of Derna. I beg to differ with your dangerous illusion. The trouble is grave, mysterious and deep.' / *Radio Times Hulton Picture Library*

Below: A 6-inch howitzer negotiating a difficult bend in the foothills of the Djebel Akhdar above Giovanni Berta. After two months' campaigning uniform has become something of a memory, and no two men are dressed alike. The 'zift' hat, seen in the foreground, was very popular throughout XIII Corps, and was made from a knitted cap comforter. / *IWM*

Above: Thermos Bombs were so called because of their resemblance to a vacuum flask. They were a type of anti-personnel mine, and were capable of severing the track of a light tank. Their presence could cause delay or restrict passage of a route forward. / *IWM*

Below: The Australian advance along the coast from Tobruk was slowed down by demolitions, but by 25 January 19th Infantry Brigade was exchanging fire with the defenders of the Wadi Derna. During the night of 28/29 January the Italians abandoned the Derna position because of indirect pressure from 7th Armoured Division to the south which threatened to isolate them in the manner of Bardia and Tobruk. Their resistance had halted 6th Australian Division, and was described as being some of the fiercest of the campaign. This M11 was discovered in the outskirts of the town, lurking coyly in a rickety shed; its presence therein remains a mystery./*IWM*

Left: During the Derna fighting, both sides had kept their armour covering their inland flanks. Graziani had by now received a reinforcement of over 100 M13s, which had been organised into an armoured brigade under the command of General Babini.

The morning of 24 January found 7th Hussars light tanks moving forward to cut the Mechili-Derna track. Shortly after 1000hrs they were assailed by 14 M13s which came on, firing on the move. Having only three cruisers with which to make effective reply, the Hussars had no alternative but to retire as quickly as possible, transmitting a call for assistance to HQ 4th Armoured Brigade, which instructed 2 RTR to intervene in the action. The Second found it difficult to accept the idea of Italian armour being handled aggressively, and underestimated the seriousness of the situation, but despatched C Squadron at 1100hrs. By this time the Hussars had lost several light tanks and a cruiser, while a second cruiser was useless with a jammed 2-pdr, although two of the enemy had been knocked out in return. Forty minutes later a Hussar officer arrived in the Second's leaguer to emphasise how hard his regiment was being pressed. He was able to indicate the position of the Italian tanks, which was radioed to C Squadron while A Squadron was scrambled and sent towards the action.

The enemy tanks were spotted on a ridge, and at 1155hrs C Squadron's cruisers opened fire from the south. Five minutes later those of A Squadron engaged from the east, and the Italians were caught in a fire-trap from which only five of their tanks escaped. The Second sustained no casualties although the range had closed to 600yd. It was revealed on examination of the M13s that the solid 2-pdr shot had passed right through, leaving a clean hole. One tank was captured in running order and despatched to 4th Armoured Brigade HQ as a trophy.

Following the decision to abandon the position at Derna, the Babini Armoured Brigade withdrew north towards the coast to cover the retreat on Benghazi. / *IWM*

Right: M13s moving in echelon to avoid each other's dust. With the exception of its brush with 7th Hussars and 2 RTR on 24 January, the Babini Armoured Brigade did not attempt to interfere with XIII Corps' operations, and was employed passively as the Italian army's flank and rear guard, although in numbers of medium tanks available for action it was potentially stronger than 7th Armoured Division. On the other hand, the brigade's lack of experience and the fact that only a handful of its tanks were fitted with radios made any sort of offensive operation in a risky business.
/ *Keystone Press Agency Ltd*

O'Connor's Trap

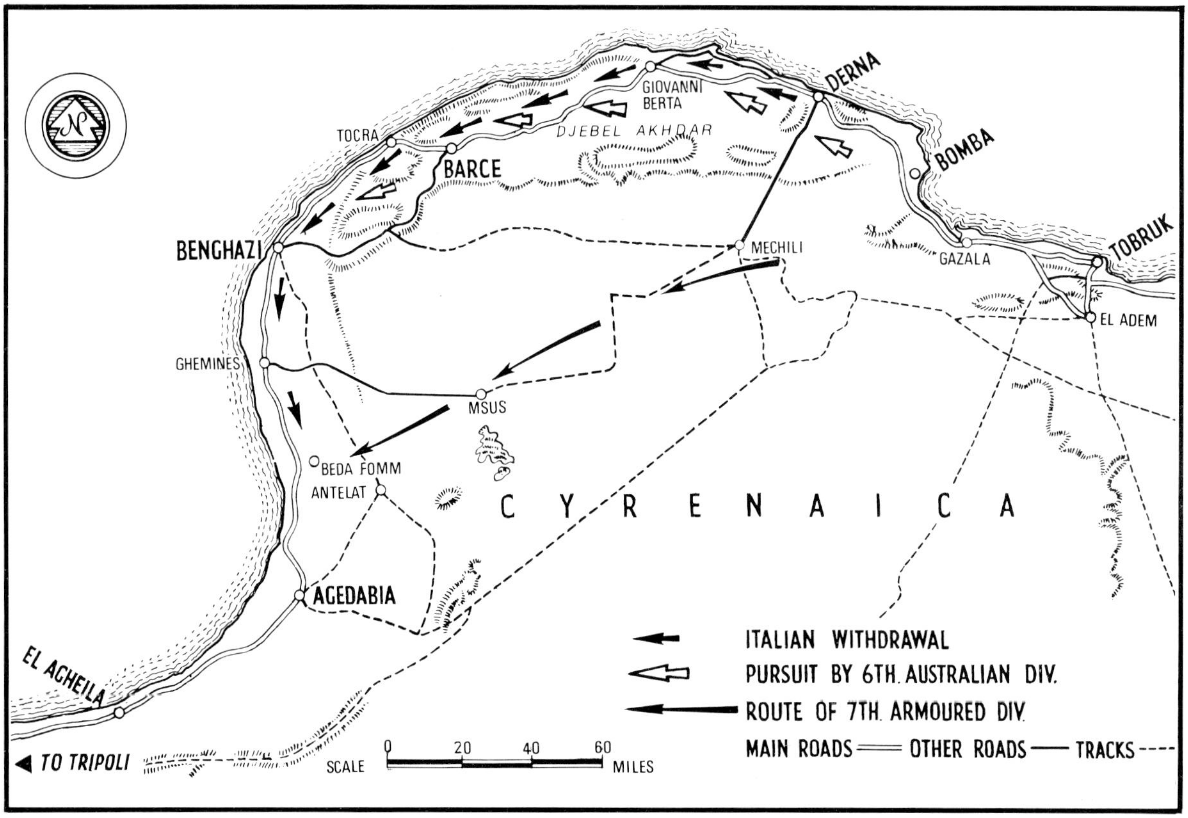

Above: O'Connor's trap. Once it became clear that the Italians were withdrawing from Derna along the coast road to Benghazi and thus north of the Djebel Akhdar, O'Connor felt that a real chance existed to entrap and destroy his opponent. His plan required 6th Australian Division to continue its pursuit along the coast, while 7th Armoured Division cut across the Benghazi bulge south of the Djebel, travelling from Mechili via Msus and Antelat to the coast near Beda Fomm, where it would go into a blocking position. If the move could be completed in time, the Italian Army would find itself trapped between XIII Corps' two major formations.

Left: The advance guard, known as Combeforce after its commander, and consisting of 11th Hussars, 2nd Rifle Brigade, C Battery 4 RHA's 25-pdrs and nine portee anti-tank guns manned by men of 106 RHA, began to move forward on 4 February. In its wake travelled 4th Armoured Brigade, now consisting of 3rd and 7th Hussars and 2nd Royal Tank Regiment, followed by 7th Armoured Brigade, reduced in strength to 1st Royal Tank Regiment only, and the Support Group. The move itself is described by Maj-Gen Ralph Younger, who commanded a 7th Hussar squadron at Beda Fomm: 'There was some very rough going early on, mainly loose slab rock, and this slowed down the pace and also increased petrol consumption. The Italians had also left a lot of thermos bombs; care had to be taken to avoid these and this again slowed down the pace. The petrol lorries were not able to keep up with the tanks, and this being before the days of jerricans, the 4-gallon containers being very flimsy, much petrol was lost through leakage. Petrol was certainly a worry. The range of the Mark VIB on this sort of going was not more than 100 miles. Although the wireless sets were often shaken off net, the operators were experienced and kept communications satisfactory. I remember that we were all pretty battered by the time we got to Beda Fomm.' / *IWM*

Above: Shortly after noon on 5 February Combeforce established a road-block on the coast road at Beda Fomm. There was barely time for the infantry to dig in and for a few mines to be laid when at 1430hrs the head of a long Italian convoy began to approach from the north.

Vehicles went up on mines and others were set ablaze by fire from the armoured cars and 25-pdr battery. The escorting Bersaglieri regiment launched a series of disconnected attacks against the block, but these were ineffective, largely because of the absence of artillery and tank support. At this stage the majority of the Italians' fighting troops were still further north, and Combeforce had merely succeeded in halting a number of administrative units that were leading the withdrawal from Benghazi.

However, during the afternoon the pressure on the road-block began to increase, and Combe suggested to Brig Caunter, commanding the fast approaching 4th Armoured Brigade, that the British tanks should engage the steadily lengthening enemy column from a series of ridges to the east of the road. Caunter agreed and as the evening drew on he threw all three regiments against the Italians' flank. Maj Younger's squadron was the first to arrive: 'At about 5pm B Squadron was ordered to find out if Beda Fomm itself, a windmill on high ground, was held. In no time at all the leading troop leader reported it clear, and that there was a long column of transport halted on the road away to the west. We knew that Combeforce was in position a few miles to the south-west, across the road. In spite of the tanks being very low on petrol B and C Squadrons attacked the column, and only darkness, partly relieved by a burning petrol tanker, saved much of it from being destroyed.' / *IWM*

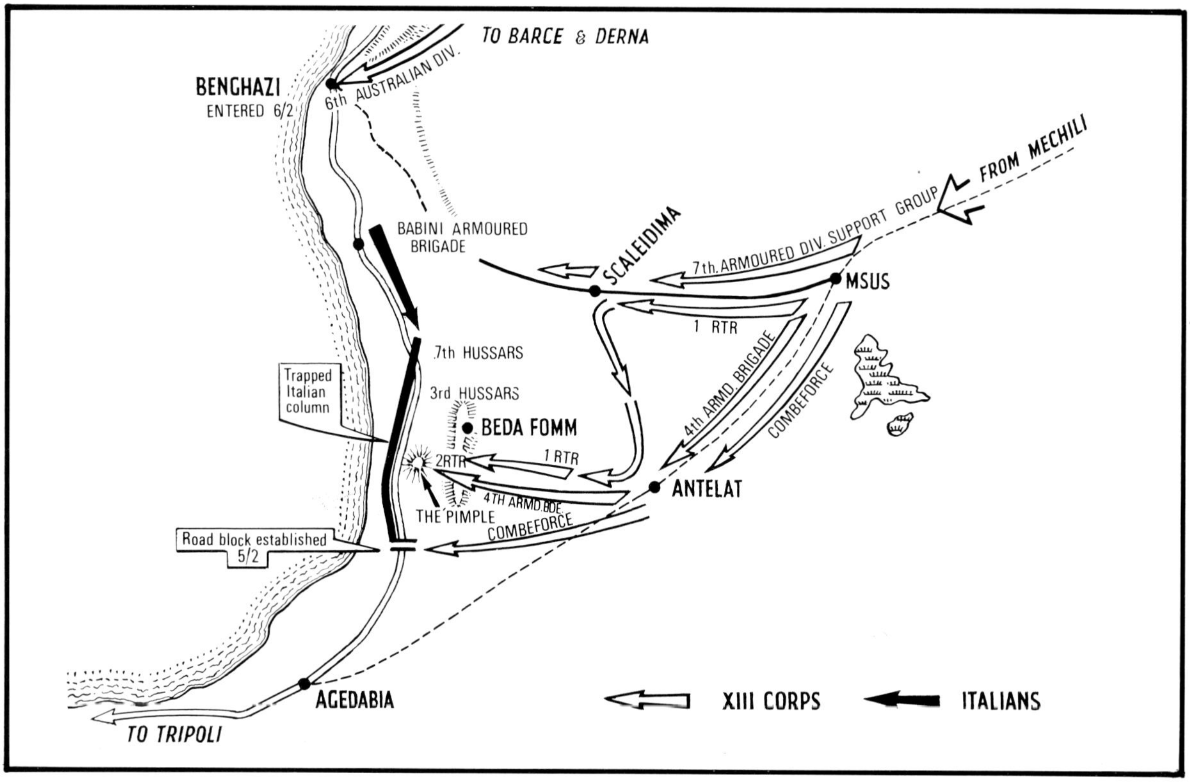

Above: The ambush at Beda Fomm 5-7 February 1941.

Right: Throughout the night a worried General Bergonzoli worked on a plan which he hoped would enable the trapped army to fight its way through the cordon of British armour. Artillery had now begun to arrive in quantity, as well as the first 60 tanks of the Babini Armoured Brigade, which had been acting as the column's rearguard.

Bergonzoli intended mounting a holding attack on Combeforce, while his tanks swung off the road at a point known as The Pimple, some miles to the north, where they would smash through the cordon before heading south to take the road-block in flank and rear.

6 February dawned windy and rain-laden. The Italian tank attack was badly coordinated and was repeatedly shot to pieces by 2 RTR's cruisers firing hull-down from ridges to the east. The photograph shows The Pimple after the action with 104/40 medium guns on the summit, still trained on the British positions. / *IWM*

Below: M13s attacking under shellfire. In spite of their lack of expertise the Italian tank men showed more determination to come to grips at Beda Fomm than at any other time during the campaign. However, the absence of radios in all but company commander's tanks (one of which can be seen on the left) meant that after an attack had been launched it was very difficult to control; in consequence, each objective had to be strictly limited, since rapid re-deployment in the British manner was an impossibility. Other reasons for the failure of the Italian armour to break through were a lack of understanding of the principles of fire and movement, and the piecemeal commitment of units as they arrived from the north throughout the day. / *RAC Tank Museum*

Centre left: Elsewhere on 6 February, the centre of the trapped column, now 11 miles long, was savaged by 3rd Hussars, while 7th Hussars closed in on its rear. To the north-east 7th Armoured Division's Support Group had levered an Italian battlegroup out of Sceleidima and were also closing in, while 6th Australian Division had entered Benghazi.

The A10 in the foreground belongs to B Squadron 2 RTR, although it carries C Squadron markings. B Squadron, it will be recalled, were attached to 3rd Hussars throughout the campaign. The crew was captured when a track was shot away, but released the following day; they were possibly the only prisoners taken by the Italians at Beda Fomm. The two M13s in the background were knocked out by a 2-pdr portee troop of 3 RHA, also attached to 3rd Hussars. / *IWM*

Bottom left: By evening, at a cost of most of their tanks, the Italians had succeeded in pushing 2 RTR back from The Pimple, and their column was beginning to move slowly south towards Combeforce's road-block.

Whilst the Second had been unable to prevent any break-out into the desert, the regiment had also sustained loss and was virtually without ammunition when the fresh 1 RTR arrived from Antelat during the evening and waded straight into the fight, fostering Italian suspicion that the British possessed ample reserves.

To the north a Morris armoured car, captured from 11th Hussars in July, was rammed with terminal results by a 7th Hussar cruiser while making a break for freedom. Only a handful of Italians succeeded in escaping by filtering past Combeforce's seaward flank after dark. / *IWM*

Left: By nightfall it was clear to Bergonzoli that his plan was not going to work and that he would have to resort to other measures. The day's fighting had reduced the Italian tank strength to a mere 30 vehicles, and it was decided to use these to batter a way through Combeforce at dawn on the 7th.

The attack, supported by a heavy artillery concentration, was pushed home hard with the M13s as usual firing on the move, contrary to the best gunnery practice. They were met by the return fire of 106 RHA's little portees, and both sides began to suffer losses. One by one the vulnerable portees were knocked out as the Italian survivors rolled through the Rifle Brigade's position, on to which the 25-pdrs of C Battery 4 RHA now directed their own fire, having first obtained permission.

That the Italians did not break through is due in large measure to the action of the solitary surviving portee. Manned by a scratch crew consisting of the anti-tank battery commander, his batman and a cook, the vehicle was driven quickly to a flank, from which position it pumped five successive rounds into five different tanks, while the Rifle Brigade's anti-tank rifles and the 25-pdrs accounted for the remainder.

The photograph shows a 2-pdr portee in action with a gutted M11 in the foreground; the tank carries a battalion commander's markings, and possibly belonged to the defunct Libyan Tank Group. / *IWM*

Centre right: Throughout the action the Rifle Brigade had stuck to their trenches and prevented the Italian infantry from following up their tanks. With the loss of the last M13s Bergonzoli's men had nothing with which to fight their way out of the trap, and soon white flags were appearing everywhere along the column as men came forward to surrender, leaving piles of abandoned equipment by the roadside. The Battle of Beda Fomm was over. / *IWM*

Bottom right: Gen Tellera, commander of the Italian Xth Army, had been mortally wounded during the fighting, but 'Electric Whiskers' Bergonzoli, seen here arriving in Cairo, surrendered to Col Combe, who gave him breakfast. Over the meal Bergonzoli, a dignified figure in spite of his unfortunate nickname, commented upon his amazement at finding the road blocked by British troops. His Staff, he said, had calculated that the British advance guard was still two days march away, and closing in on Benghazi. / *IWM*

Above: O'Connor remarked that he had seldom seen such a scene of wreckage and confusion as existed along the line of the trapped column, which Arabs were already beginning to loot. In places smashed lorries, bodies, abandoned tanks and guns lay in a formless jumble indicative of the growing despair of men who have seen their freedom snatched from them at the last moment. Over 25,000 prisoners were taken, as well as 1,500 wheeled vehicles, 216 guns and over 100 tanks, of which sufficient remained in working order to re-equip the entire 6th Royal Tank Regiment.

The Italian Army in North Africa had been utterly destroyed, and O'Connor despatched a short but intelligible message to Wavell to signal the event; it read simply, 'Fox killed in the open.' / *IWM*

Below: The Australians entered Benghazi on 6 February, somewhat surprised to be hailed by the civic dignitaries as 'gallant Allies'. When the airfield was captured it was found that no attempt had been made to destroy these fighter bombers or other types of aircraft which were temporarily unserviceable. The open cowlings, abandoned tool boxes and overturned steps all suggest a hurried departure by the ground crews. / *IWM*

Above: A Morris armoured car of the King's Dragoon Guards, who had relieved 11th Hussars, moving south along the Tripoli road past the wreckage of Beda Fomm. The long advance halted at a bottleneck between a salt marsh and the sea, known as El Agheila. It would be two years before a British army advanced into Tripolitania, and in the meantime the sands of the Western Desert would soak up the blood and treasure of the British, German and Italian Armies in a struggle which crossed and re-crossed the old battlefields and ranged further afield still. The question will always be asked, could such a struggle have been avoided if XIII Corps had continued its advance to Tripoli? And since it did not, were not is victories hollow in the light of future events?

Between El Agheila and Tripoli lay only a single Italian division and such remnants as had been able to escape the debacle in Cyrenaica. Within XIII Corps the Australians were begging to be allowed to continue, while 7th Armoured Division could have replenished its stocks with captured vehicles. Could XIII Corps have got to Tripoli? In Sir Richard O'Connor's words:
'I think we could have done so at once, or fairly shortly after, before the Luftwaffe came into the picture. Of course, the question of supplies would have been difficult. But this would have been greatly eased by the Italian rations which we could have picked up at Sirte and Tripoli. Like the rest of the campaign it would have been a risk, but I think personally not a dangerous one.'
Should the attempt have been made? Hindsight returns an unequivocal yes, but hindsight is a distorting mirror and does not always reflect the conditions in which decisions are made. Wavell was not fighting to acquire territory; his object from the outset had been the destruction of the Italian Army, and the last act in that drama had been played at Beda Fomm. His prime consideration now was the despatch of troops to the aid of the hard pressed Greeks, and, as the Italians in Tripolitania posed no threat, his decision to leave only a covering force at El Agheila is militarily justifiable. He firmly believed that the campaign in Greece stood a reasonable chance of success. O'Connor has commented that had he had the slightest inkling of what was to follow, he would have continued his advance until he received firm and definite orders to halt.

Few on either side would have ventured to predict that within weeks it would be the British who were in disorderly retreat. When Maj-Gen Erwin Rommel flew into Tripoli ahead of his troops on 12 February he held a very limited brief; to provide technical assistance and advice for the Italians with a view to *their* eventually mounting a campaign for the recovery of Cyrenaica. It could not have been foreseen that the following month he would in effect disobey those orders and, having probed the British lines and found a weakness, exploit it ruthlessly. On hearing the news, Halder, the German Army Chief of General Staff, exploded angrily that Rommel was 'a dangerous lunatic and must be stopped.' Only his astonishing success saved Rommel from disgrace.

To what extent, then, should XIII Corps' victories be regarded as wasted? In material terms, O'Connor's men had destroyed no less than 10 Italian divisions, taken over 130,000 prisoners, captured 380 tanks and 845 guns, and advanced more than 500 miles, at a cost of only 500 dead, 1,373 wounded, 55 missing, and a handful of tanks written off; this in itself is a staggering achievement.

The campaign had also underlined to a greater degree than the Italian defeats in Greece that Mussolini's war machine was incapable of fighting a mechanised war, and it committed German support irrevocably to the Italian cause. Before Operation Compass, the Italians had refused German aid on the grounds that it might provoke a British offensive; in late December 1940, Hitler, on the advice of his generals who already regarded the war in Africa as lost, smoothly rejected the Duce's request for German tanks on the grounds that they were unsuitable for tropical use. It was the series of defeats in Cyrenaica, inflicted on a scale and at a speed which had not been considered possible, that caused Hitler to change his mind, since they spelled political extinction for Mussolini unless something was done. Thereafter, as in World War I, Germany found herself 'shackled to a corpse'.

In the wider sphere, Franco duly noted the discomfiture of his former benefactor, and announced that Spain would remain neutral; a suggestion that German troops be allowed passage through Spain for an attack on Gibraltar was rejected. His debt to the Axis dictators was paid by the despatch of 'volunteers' to the Eastern Front.

The Battle of Britain had shown the world that the British intended to fight on in defence of their homeland; Wavell's victory showed that they could also hit back and win. It also showed that, given proper leadership, British armour could achieve the same success as the much vaunted panzer divisions, who were, after all, simply acting on British tactical concepts. Such victories cannot be described as wasted. / *IWM*

Fighting Vehicles

Light Tank Mark VIB

Weight: 5.2 tons
Crew: Commander, Gunner, Driver
Armament: Vickers .303in mg and one Vickers .50in mg
Armour: 14mm max
Engine: Meadows 88hp
Speed: 35mph
Length: 12ft 11.5in
Width: 6ft 9in
Height: 7ft 3.5in

The Light Tank Mark VI series began to enter service in 1936 as the mount of the mechanised cavalry regiments. While fast and photogenic, the vehicles offered little protection to their crews, and it is on record that the occupants of one Mark VIB, penetrated at Arras, plugged the entry and exit holes with 'a very smelly pair of socks', which at least kept the daylight out. When the Light Tank series was originally conceived, there was a feeling that tanks would not engage each other on the battlefield; the Battle of France proved that this idea was completely without foundation, and the Lights suffered severely. Against an army as ill-equipped as that of the Italians in North Africa, they could hold their own and even inflict damage, relying on their speed to get them

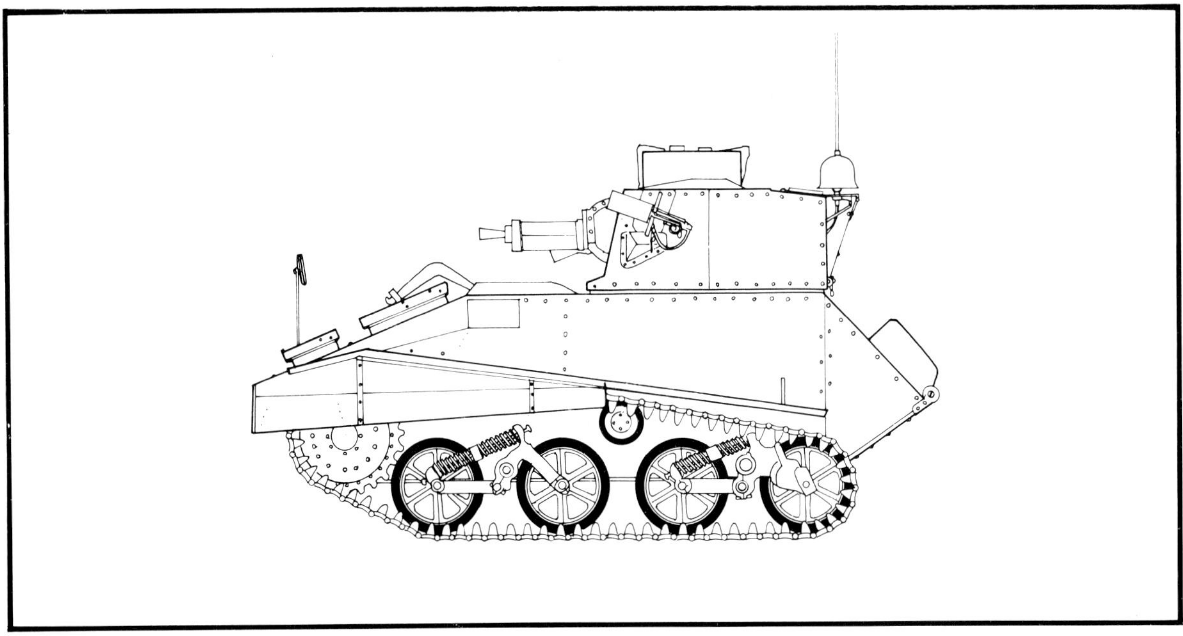

out of trouble if necessary, although, as we have seen, this did not always save them. Above a certain speed their transmission could give rise to an alarming phenomenon known as reversed steering, which could send the tank in exactly the opposite direction to that desired. The final development in this series was the Mark VIC, which carried medium and heavy Besa machine guns in place of the Vickers.

This 'early days' photograph (*left*) shows a full set of vehicle markings on the nearest tank, which belongs to No 1 Troop, A Squadron, 3rd King's Own Hussars. The famous jerboa has not yet entered the white circle of the divisional sign, but the 6-ton bridge classification has been painted on to a stowage box on the glacis plate. The sand guards were fitted for Middle Eastern use; other points of interest are the prominent aerial base for the W/S No 11, and the AA mounting.

The Vickers Light Tank series was withdrawn from active service in late 1941, but were employed as training machines until the following year. / *IWM*

Cruiser Tank Mark I (A9)

Weight: 12 tons
Crew: Commander, Gunner, Loader/Operator, Driver 2×Auxiliary Turret Gunners
Armament: One 2-pdr gun, three .303in Vickers mg (one mounted coaxially with the 2-pdr, and one in each auxiliary turret)
Armour: 14mm
Engine: AEC 150hp petrol
Speed: 25mph
Length: 19ft 3in
Width: 8ft 4in
Height: 8ft 8in

Originally classed as a medium tank, the A9 was designed as a replacement for the ageing Vickers Medium, and as an alternative to the expensive A6 '16-tonner' which had been abandoned on the grounds of cost. However, by the time it entered service in 1937, the A9 had been re-classified as a cruiser tank, since British policy favoured the parallel development of heavily armoured tanks for infantry support, and lighter tanks, to be known as cruisers, for general duties with the armoured divisions.

The twin auxiliary turrets had been inherited from the A6, and were manned if sufficient crew were available; otherwise they provided additional stowage space. The A9 was the first British tank to have a power traverse fitted to its turret, and its 'slow motion' suspension and much mechanical detail were also used on the A10 Cruiser tank and the very successful Valentine Infantry tank. Only 125 A9s were built, the survivors remaining in service until late 1941. This front view (*below*) shows a fully crewed and stowed A9 of 6 RTR. / *IWM*

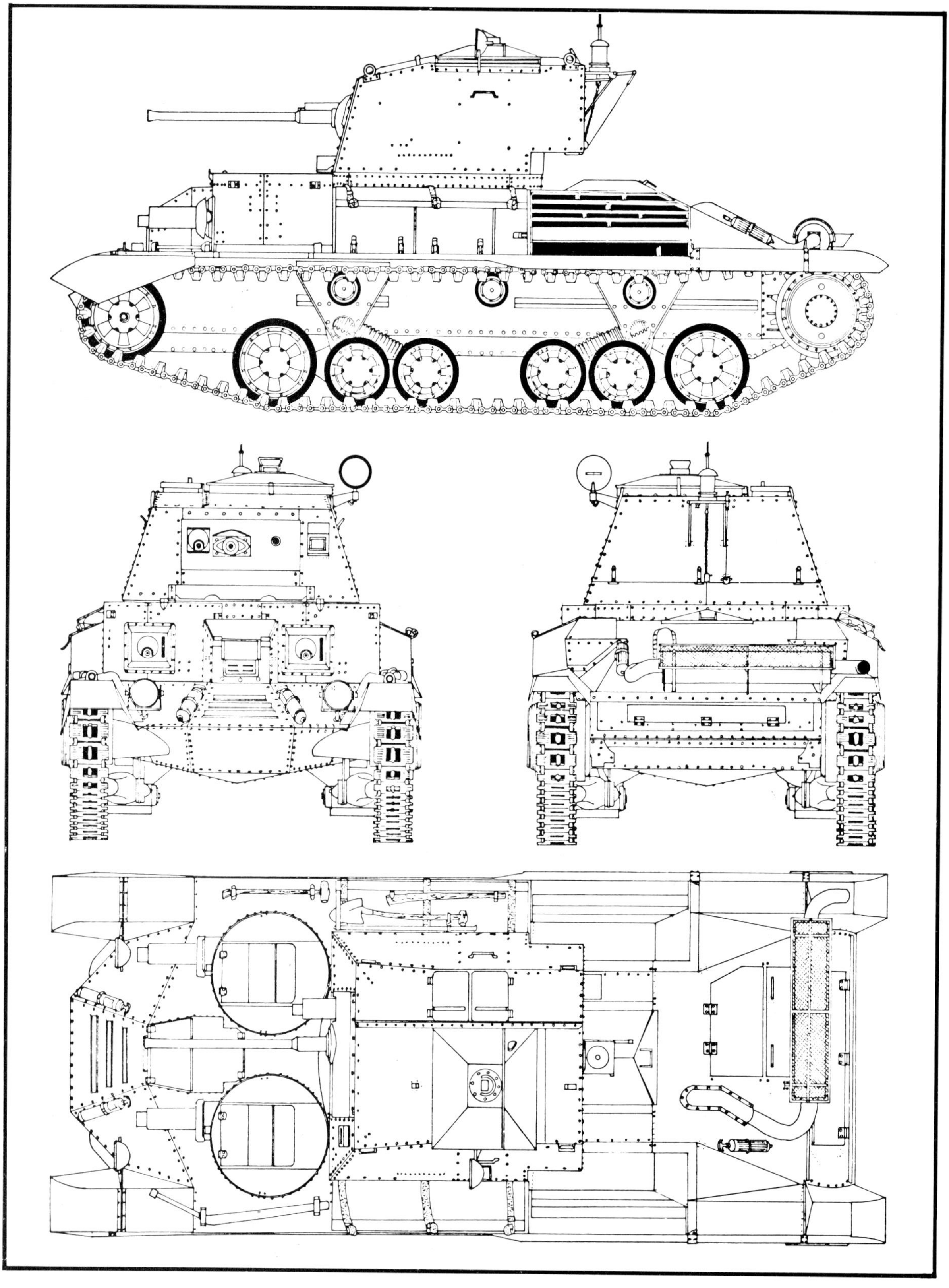

Cruiser Tank Mark II (A10)

Weight: 13.75 tons
Crew: Commander, Gunner, Loader/Operator, Driver (plus Hull Gunner in Mark IIA)
Armament: One 2-pdr gun, one .303in Vickers mg coaxially mounted (Mark II)
One 2-pdr gun, two 7.92mm Besa mg (Mark IIA)
Armour: 30mm
Engine: AEC 150hp petrol
Speed: 16mph
Length: 18ft 1in
Width: 8ft 3.5in
Height: 8ft 8in

The A10 was designed as an infantry support version of the A9, the additional armour thickness being achieved by abandoning the auxiliary turrets and bolting extra plates to the hull. However, by the time the A10 was ready for production, revised estimates of the armour required by an Infantry tank had resulted in work being started on the Matilda, and as the A10 fell well below this requirement it was re-classified as a heavy cruiser, although its speed was only 1mph faster than that of the Matilda.

This meant that the A10 fell between two stools. It was insufficiently armoured to perform the 'I' tank role, and its low speed made it incompatible with the faster A9s and A13s. In the Mark IIA version, the coaxial Vickers was replaced by a Besa mg, and provision made for the mounting of a further Besa in the front plate, as shown.

The A10 was regarded as a stop-gap vehicle pending the appearance of the A13, and its production run of 175 was completed in September 1940. It was withdrawn from service about a year later. / *IWM*

Cruiser Tanks Mark IV and IVA (A13)

Weight: 14.75 tons
Crew: Commander, Gunner, Loader/Operator, Driver
Armament: One 2-pdr, one .303in Vickers coax mg, replaced by 7.92mm coax mg on Mark IVA
Armour: 30mm
Engine: Nuffield Liberty 340hp
Speed: 30mph
Length: 19ft 9in
Width: 8ft 4in
Height: 8ft 6in

The A13 was the first of a long line of British Cruiser tanks to employ the Christie suspension. In September 1936 Lt-Col G. le Q. Martel, Assistant Director of Mechanisation, attended the Red Army manoeuvres and was impressed by the performance of the Russian BT series. On his return home he arranged for a Christie tank to be purchased privately by the Morris organisation, who then carried out the design work, which was influenced by Hobart's specification for a cruiser tank contained in his report on the 1936 Tank Brigade exercises. The result was the Cruiser Tank Mark III, which carried a turret similar to that of the A10, and was protected by 14mm armour. The Mark IV followed the same layout, but protection was increased to 30mm and a new turret with undercut sides fitted, providing the additional benefit of space between the outer plates and turret wall proper, a device employed to defeat armour piercing rounds without resorting to thick and consequently heavy armour.

The Cruiser Tank Mark IVA had an improved transmission and mantlet, the Vickers coaxial machine gun being replaced by a Besa. This frontal view (*overleaf*) shows a Mark IV flanked by two Mark IVAs.

A total of 335 A13s of all marks was produced. Like the A9 and A10, they were withdrawn from service in late 1941, having been replaced by the Cruiser Tank Mark VI (A15) Crusader and the American Stuart. / *IWM*

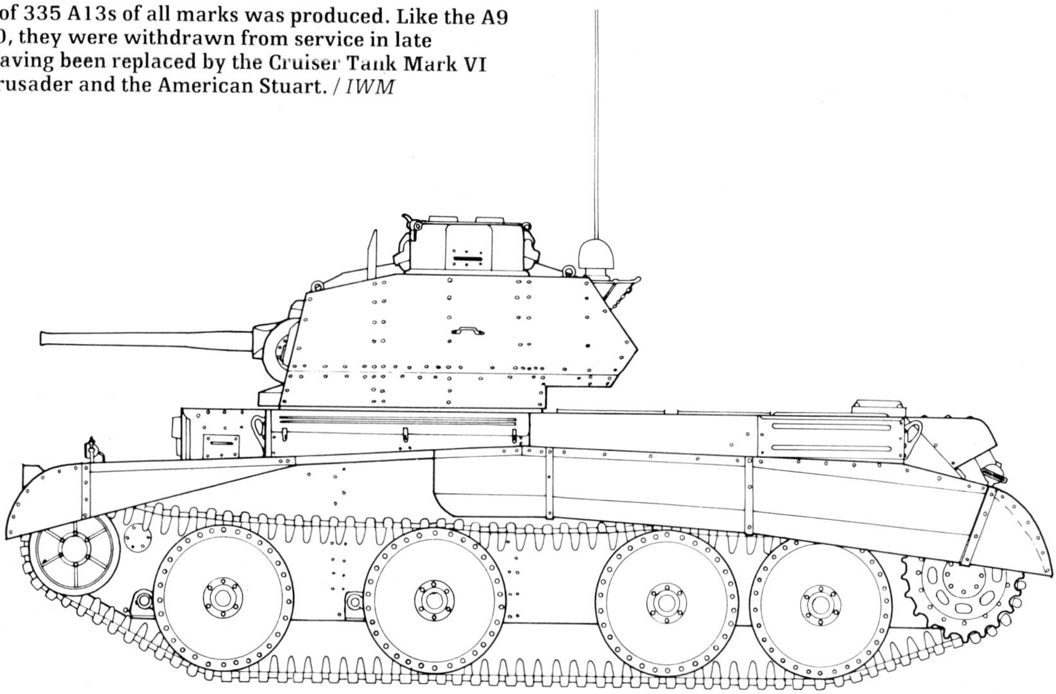

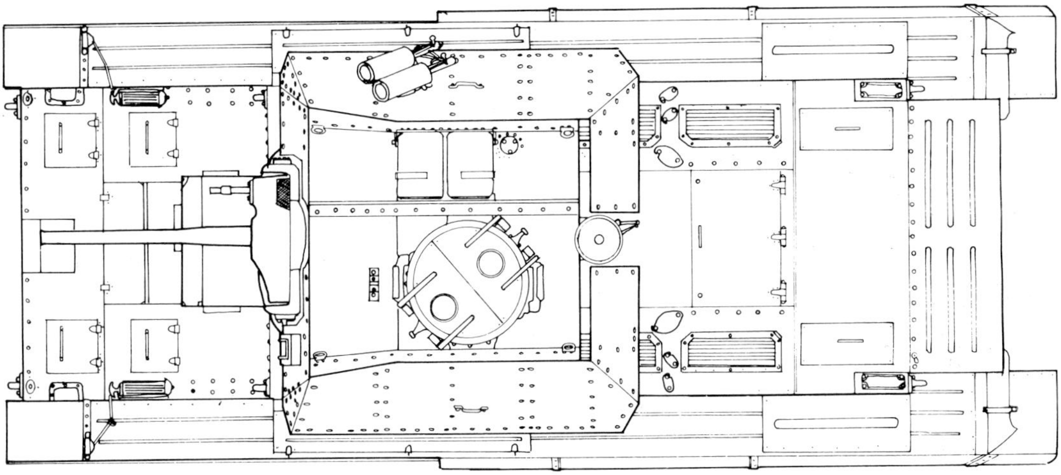

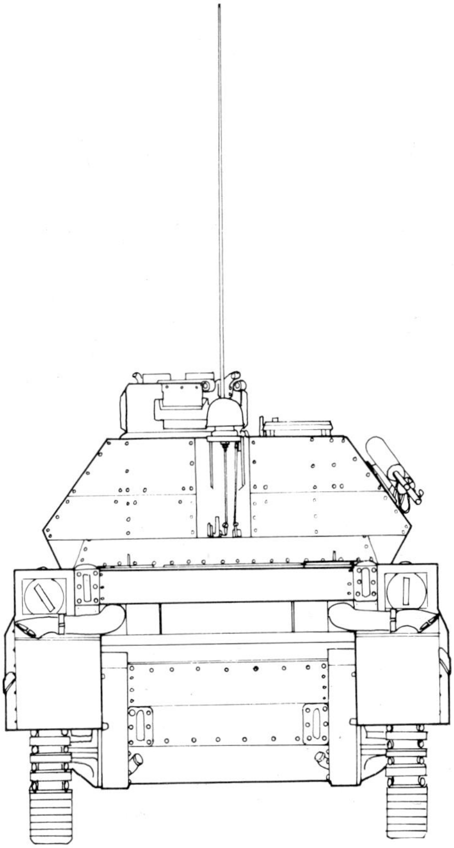

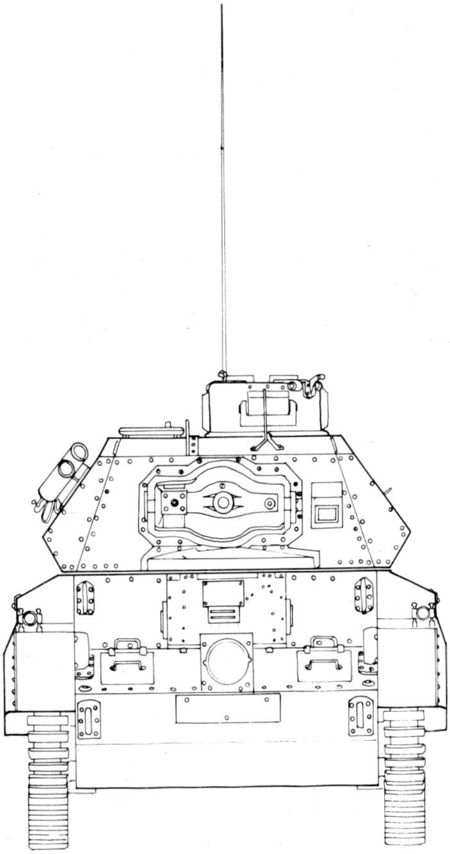

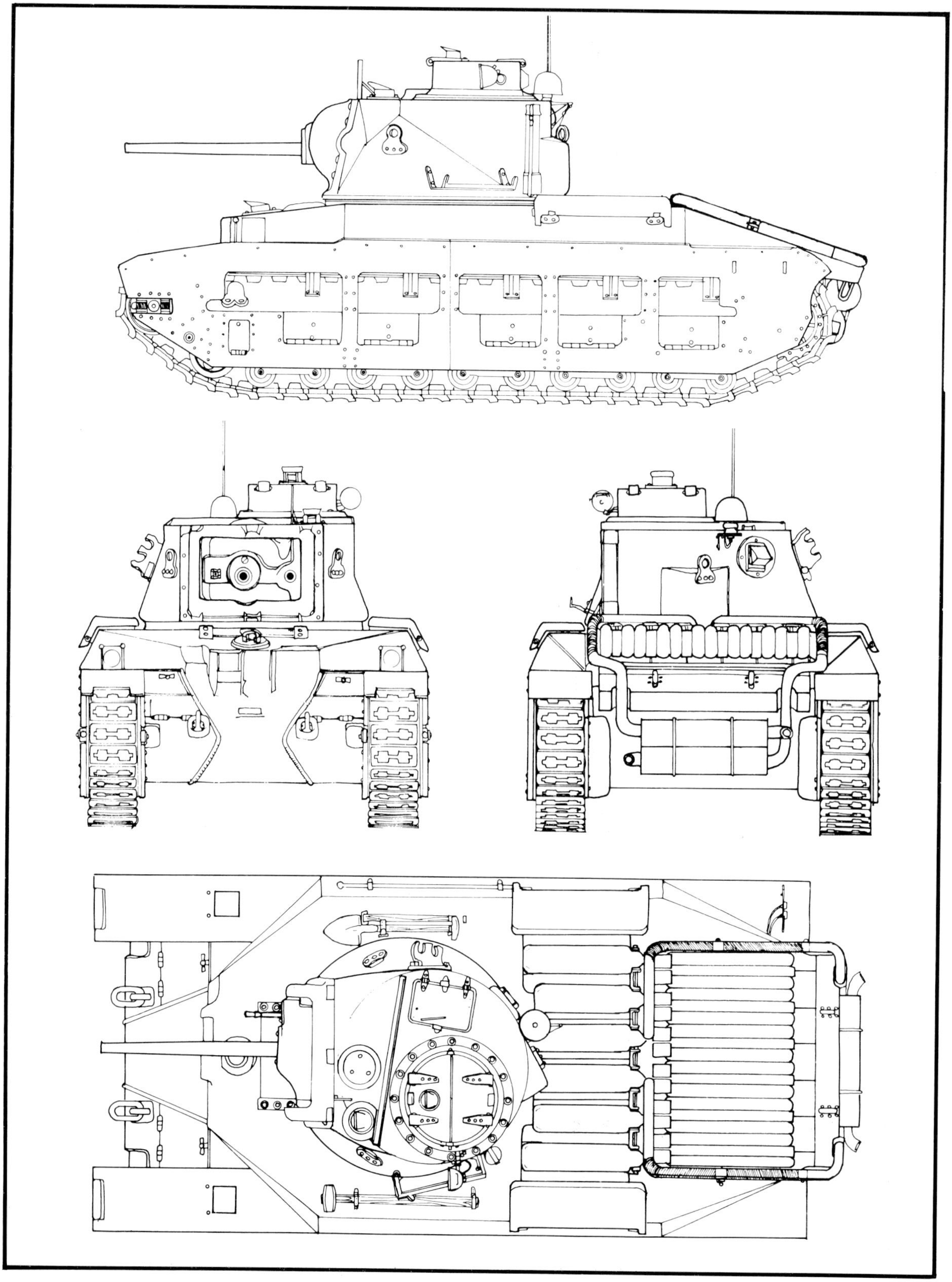

Infantry Tank Mark II (A12) Matilda

Weight: 26.5 tons
Crew: Commander, Gunner, Loader/Operator, Driver
Armament: One 2-pdr gun, one 7.92mm Besa mg, mounted coaxially
Armour: 78mm
Engines: Two AEC Diesels, total hp 174
Two Leyland Diesels, total hp 190, on later Marks
Speed: 15mph
Length: 18ft 5in (19ft 9in with auxiliary fuel tank)
Width: 8ft 6in
Height: 8ft 0in

The Matilda had been designed to withstand any anti-tank gun known to be in service, and was the second tank to carry the name into battle, the first being the smaller Infantry Tank Mark I (A11), alongside which it had fought at Arras.

In their first encounters with the Queen of the Battlefield, as the tank had become known, the Germans fared as badly as had the Italians. During the fighting around Halfaya Pass in mid-1941, startling losses were inflicted on both panzer divisions, and officers were court-martialled or lost their appointments because they were unwilling to close with the Matildas. Over 100 powerful Marder III tank destroyers were sent to North Africa to deal with the problem, but it was the deadly 88mm anti-aircraft gun, firing in the anti-tank role, that ended the Queen's reign. By the end of July 1942 the last Matilda gun tank had been withdrawn from service in North Africa, although Matildas continued to support the Australian Army's operations in the Far East. On the debit side, the Matilida was a complicated vehicle to construct, had poor steering clutches, and could not be fitted with a larger gun, although a Close Support version, mounting a 3-inch howitzer, was produced./ *IWM*

Morris Armoured Car

Weight: 4.2 tons
Crew: Commander, Gunner, Radio Operator, Driver
Armament: One Boys anti-tank rifle, one Bren lmg, one smoke grenade discharger
Armour: 7mm
Engine: Morris Commercial 96.2bhp
Speed: 45mph
Length: 15ft 7.5in
Width: 6ft 8.5in
Height: 7ft 3in

These vehicles were constructed on a commercial 15cwt chassis and had a conventional rear wheel drive. On soft going their performance was better than that of the Rolls-Royce armoured cars, but on hard rocky

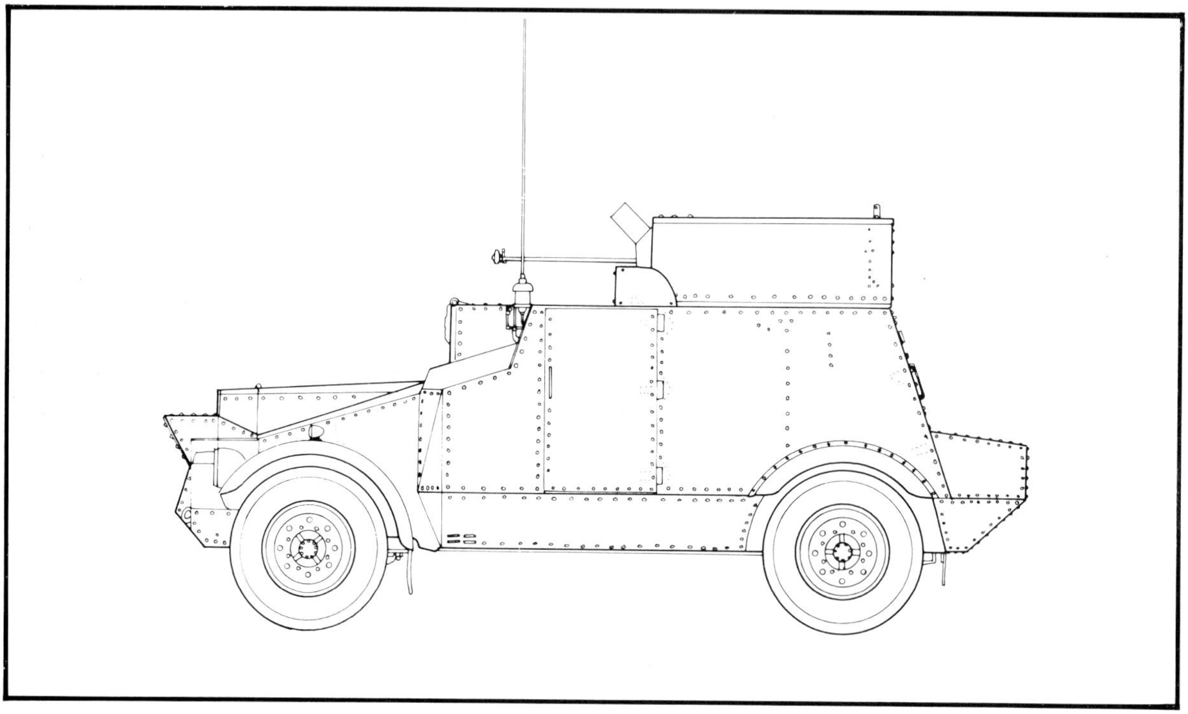

ground was not as good. Their roomy interior made them very suitable for regimental and squadron command vehicles and, as shown, a folding map table could be set up by the side door, within easy reach of the radio. The sun-shade reflects the sensible philosophy that there is no virtue in enduring discomfort for its own sake. The Morris was withdrawn from service in the spring of 1941. / *IWM*

Carrier, Scout

Weight: 4 tons
Crew: Commander, Gunner, Driver
Armament: One Boys anti-tank rifle, one Bren lmg
Armour: 12mm
Engine: Ford 65hp
Speed: 30mph
Length: 12ft 0in
Width: 6ft 11in
Height: 4ft 6in

The Carrier Scout was one of a number of very similar tracked carriers performing a variety of functions with the British and Commonwealth armies, and had been designed as a light reconnaissance vehicle for use by divisional cavalry regiments. It was carried on a Horstmann type suspension like that of the Light Tank series and shared the same fault of reverse steering at speed. This example (*right*) belonging to 6th Australian Divisional Cavalry Regiment, whose divisional sign, a kangaroo, can be seen on the nearside track-guard, is seen near Giovanna Berta, where Italian colonists had succeeded in turning areas of desert into farmland. The carrier family continued to give good service throughout the war. / *IWM*

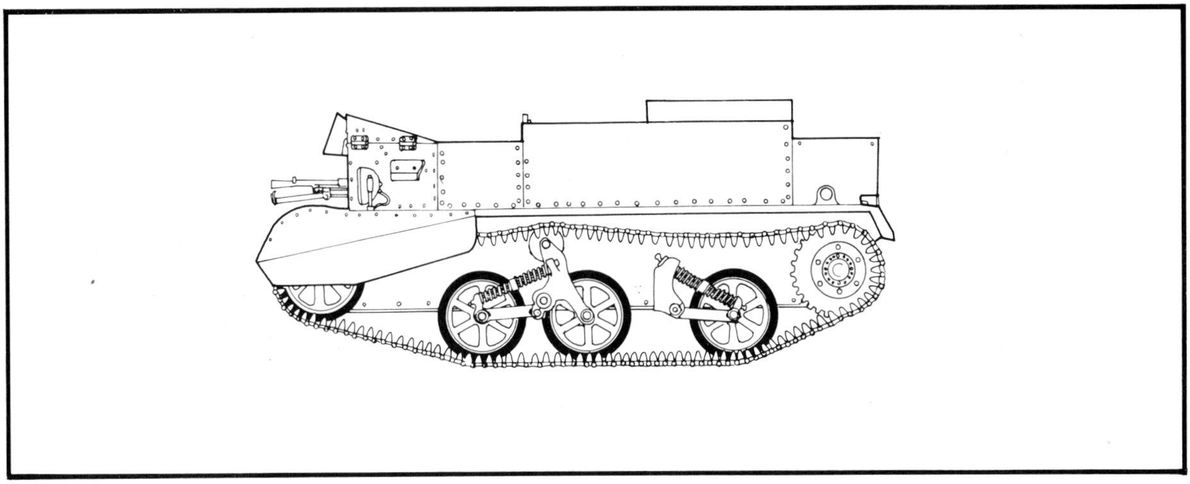

Below: The 2-pdr portee anti-tank gun. British anti-tank gunners, forced initially to tow their little 2-pdrs over all sorts of bad going, found that the constant battering was impairing their weapons' efficiency. The answer appeared in the shape of the portee, said to be the invention of a Rhodesian officer, Lt Gillson.

The gun was mounted on the back of a cut-down lorry, and the idea was that it would be carried piggy-back into action and then dismounted for use; in fact the gun was rarely dismounted, first because time would not permit, and secondly because the ammunition was stowed in bins behind the mounting and would have to be unloaded for ground firing.

Whilst the portee conferred greater mobility it suffered from serious disadvantages; first, the gun had only the same range as contemporary tank guns when, ideally, an anti-tank weapon should out-range that of its opponent; and second, of course, the detachment was terribly vulnerable.

During the campaign the 2-pdr portee was used by 3 RHA, and an officer of this regiment, Lt Ward Gunn, was awarded a posthumous Victoria Cross when his troop beat off a German massed tank attack during the fighting at Sidi Rezegh in November 1941. / *IWM*

Right: The slightly less powerful 37mm Bofors anti-tank gun was also carried portee, and was used by 106 RHA. Its distinctive gun-shield makes it easily identifiable. The 37mm was withdrawn from service early in 1941. / *IWM*

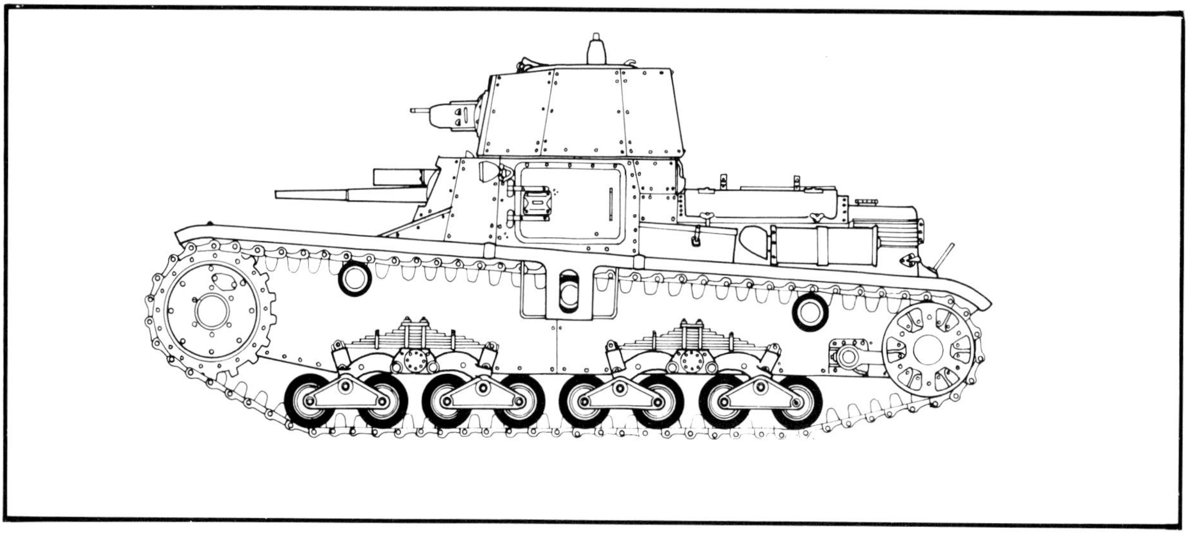

M11/39 Medium Tank

Weight: 10.8 tons
Crew: Commander, Gunner/Loader, Driver
Armament: One 37mm gun in hull, two 8mm mg in turret
Armour: 30mm max
Engine: Fiat SPA 8T V-8 105hp
Speed: 21mph
Length: 15ft 6.5in
Width: 7ft 2in
Height: 7ft 4.5in

A very poor design which allowed only a limited traverse of the main armament. The internal layout was also unsatisfactory, as the commander and gunner/loader were placed at different levels and communication between them was difficult. / *IWM*

M13/M40 Medium Tank

Weight: 13.5 tons
Crew: Commander/Gunner, Loader, Hull Gunner, Driver
Armament: One 47mm gun plus one 8mm coax mg in turret and two 8mm mg in hull
Armour: 30mm max
Engine: Fiat SPA 8T V-8 105hp
Speed: 19mph
Length: 16ft 1.5in
Width: 7ft 4in
Height: 7ft 10in

The M13 corrected many of the faults found in the M1, but the commander's doing double duty as gunner was not a desirable feature and can only have worked to the detriment of both functions. The basic M13 design remained in service throughout the war.

These examples (*below*) captured at Beda Fomm, show a clear set of markings for 1st, 2nd and 3rd Platoons of No 1 Company, and almost certainly belonged to a battalion of 132nd Ariete Armoured Regiment, which had been forced to send many of its tanks to Libya to replace the catastrophic losses earlier in the campaign; one tank, however, shows the sign of the Vth Battalion, which formed part of the 32nd Centauro Armoured Regiment. Italian company markings consisted of painted oblongs, red for No 1, sky blue for No 2, and yellow for No 3. The number of white bars refers to the platoon, and the numeral above to the tank itself. Thus, the tank in the foreground is the third vehicle of No 1 Company's 2nd Platoon. Battalion markings, in Roman characters, often appeared on the rear of the fighting compartment. The white circle on the turret top is intended for aerial identification, and the saloon cars in the background carry a similar device. / *IWM*

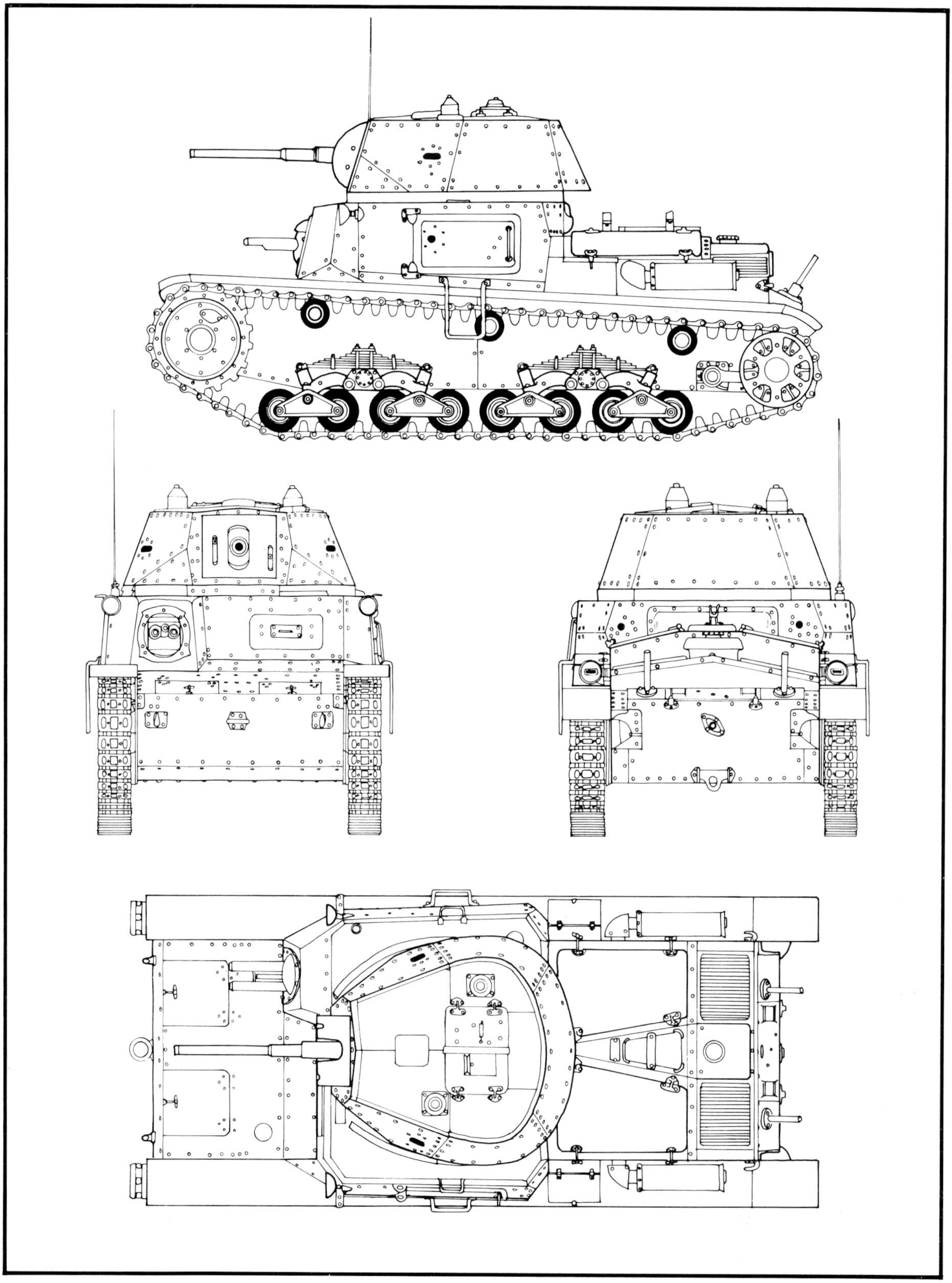

L3 Light Tank

(sometimes referred to as the CV3: CV=Carro Veloce, or Fast Tank)
Weight: 3.4 tons
Crew: Commander/Gunner, Driver
Armament: One 6.5mm mg or two 8mm mg
Armour: 13.5mm max
Engine: Fiat SPA CV3 43hp
Speed: 26mph
Length: 12ft 7in
Width: 4ft 0in
Height: 4ft 3in

In spite of its thin armour, the L3 had been designed for infantry support, primarily in mountainous areas. It had performed this function in Ethiopia, but by 1940 could not seriously be regarded as anything more than a protected weapons carrier, although it was the most numerous type of AFV in North Africa and equipped the organic tank battalions of the Italian infantry divisions. This vehicle (*bottom*) was knocked out early in the campaign by a Boys anti-tank rifle, and is being examined by men of the 11th Hussars. / *IWM*

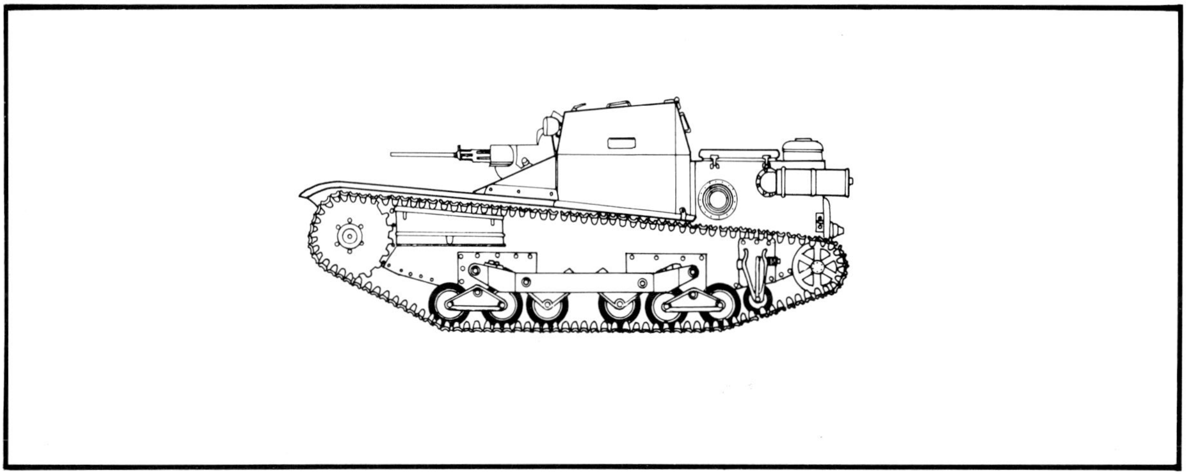

Below: The basic chassis of the L3 also provided a small artillery tractor. These vehicles and their towed 100/17 howitzers failed to make their escape from the trap at Buq Buq. / *IWM*

Below and top right: In the Autoblinda AB40/41 series the Italian Army had better all-round armoured cars than the Rolls-Royce and Morris machines possessed by the British. The early pattern of turret, mounting twin 8mm Breda machine guns, was replaced by the L6 light tank turret containing a 20mm cannon and a coaxial 8mm machine gun, as seen in these examples. A further machine gun was carried in the hull. Maximum armour thickness was 15mm. The three-man ABs could achieve 48mph on roads and had a good cross-country performance as well.

Unfortunately, these qualities were not employed to their best effect, since the Italians did not use their armoured cars as aggressively as the British, preferring to employ them as escorts and as transport for senior officers in forward areas, and relying on the Reggia Aeronautica for reconnaissance. / *RAC Tank Museum*

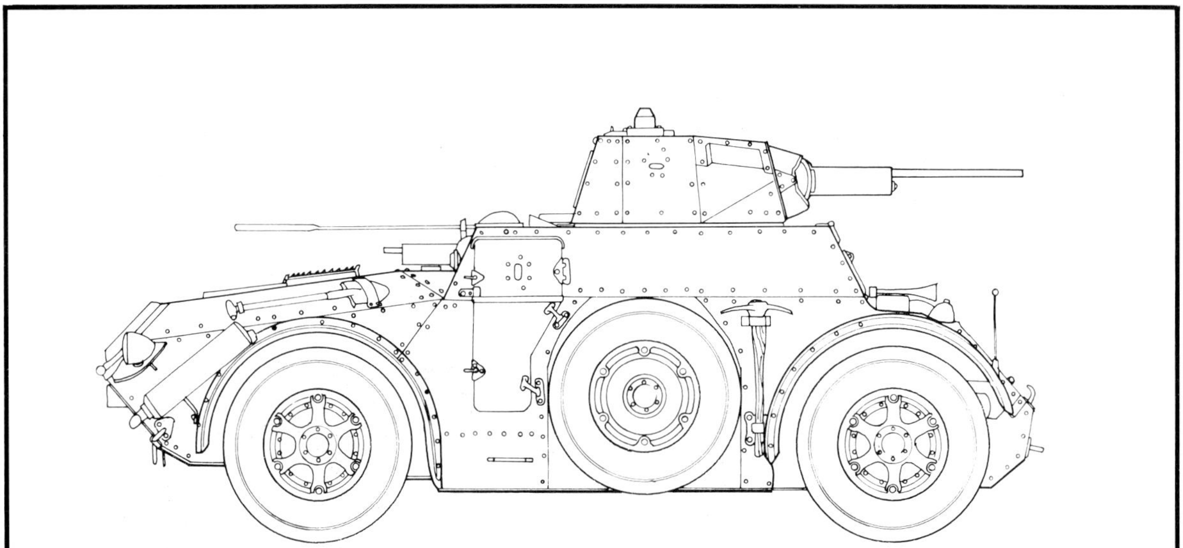

Below: If some of the British armoured cars might have been considered to be a little elderly, several of their opponents fell into the vintage class. These Bianchi cars, captured in Cyrenaica, almost certainly date from World War I, and have many points of similarity with the Bianchis employed in Libya during Italo-Turkish wars of 1912, the first campaign in which automotive AFVs were used. As originally built, the cars had enclosed turrets. They were manned by a crew of three (sometimes four) and protected by 6mm armour plate. A single machine gun was carried. On good going they could achieve about 20mph, but by 1940 they had outlived their usefulness as front line combat vehicles, and had possibly been handed over to the police for internal security duties. / *IWM*